TOP TENS

DIYS

CHALLENGES

VLOGS, TAGS & HAULS

CONTENTS

▶ ▶ GENERATION

YouTube has come a long way since the very first video was uploaded to the site in 2005. Nowadays, more people are logging on and watching content than ever before, with over 300 hours of video being uploaded to the site every minute. This is the year that YouTubers have finally been accepted as proper celebrities in the real world, with book deals, TV appearances and millions of fans following their every move. Millions more are being inspired to create their own channels too: shooting, uploading and sharing new videos in an ever-growing creative community.

One thing's for sure – whether we're creating our own content or simply streaming our favourite stars, we just love to entertain ourselves with the wonderful world of YouTube.

YouTube is the third most visited site on the Internet, behind Google and Facebook.

YOUTUBE

JOIN THE VLOG SQUAD!

From fashion to fitness, food recipes to music parodies, book reviews to confidence tips and everything in between, vloggers touch on literally every content category you can think of.

With so many channels to choose from, it can be hard to know where to start. This book will help you find great channels to watch, whether you're all about travel, a budding fashionista, a fitness fanatic or a beauty star, or even if you just fancy a YouTube binge sesh. We've scoured the Internet to bring you the biggest and best YouTube gurus as well as some up-and-coming stars to add to your subscription box. This is your ultimate guide for what to watch on the web. Plus, you'll learn about vlogging styles, find out what the top trending tags are and pick up tips and tricks from those in the know to get your very own channel started. Could you be the next vlogging superstar?

FASHION MUSIC DIY

LIFESTYLE FOOD

BEAUTY TRAVEL

BOOKS FITNESS

CRAFTS ADVICE

FASH TAGS

YouTube style stars have made it easier than ever to access fashion, with just the click of a button. As well as being super stylish, they're also incredibly inventive; filming a variety of different videos to keep their viewers connected. Here are some of the most popular tags.

WHAT MAKES A FASHION VLOGGER?

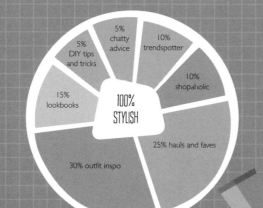

- 5% chatty advice
- 10% trendspotter
- 5% DIY tips and tricks
- 10% shopaholic
- 15% lookbooks
- 100% STYLISH
- 25% hauls and faves
- 30% outfit inspo

WHAT'S IN MY BAG?

> > > > > > > > > > > > > >

WHAT IS IT: The 'What's in my bag' videos are exactly what they sound like: a vlogger pulls items out of their bag one-by-one and talks about them. From essential cosmetics, electronics, pretty purses and even the bag itself, the content of this video is whatever you carry around with you.

WATCH IT FOR: A quick way to get to know your faves. Fans love this type of video as they are just like haul vlogs; it introduces them to new products, as well as getting a little more insight into their favourite YouTuber's life.

HOW TO: These are incredibly popular and are a mix of personal information and product reviews. Hint: keep it brief – there's only so long you can talk about a key chain for, and there's only so long people will want to listen.

WATCH:

> > > > > > > > > > > > > >

WE <3 Claire Marshall's unique take on a 'What's in my bag?' video:

Claire Marsh...
846564

HERE ARE SOME OTHER VARIATIONS YOU COULD TRY:

WHAT'S ON MY PHONE (APPS)?
WHAT'S IN MY FRIDGE?
WHAT'S IN MY DRAWER?
WHAT'S IN MY LOCKER?
WHAT'S IN MY MAKE-UP BAG?

Or why not be a trendsetter and come up with your own!

OUTFIT OF THE DAY (OOTD)

>>>>>>>>>>>>>>

WHAT IS IT: OOTD videos show off a vlogger's daily fashion look, sometimes for a special occasion. Like lookbooks, these videos are usually highly stylised and include details of how the viewer can recreate the look.

WATCH IT FOR: Serious style inspiration to shake up your wardrobe. Fashion vloggers will often put things together in ways you wouldn't have dreamed of. Seeing the clothes on somebody else can also help give you the confidence to try something new or different.

HOW TO: A good fashion vlogger shows every outfit from every angle, with close-up details and full-length shots. A great OOTD shows the clothes at their best and leaves viewers excited to create their own looks with the key pieces.

YOU CAN ALSO FILM YOUR DAILY LOOK EVERY DAY FOR A WEEK TO MAKE AN OUTFIT OF THE WEEK VIDEO!

DIY

>>>>>>>>>>>>>>

WHAT IS IT: Fashion DIY (Do It Yourself) YouTubers use simple steps and inexpensive materials to show viewers how to create almost anything, from Halloween costumes to candles, dresses and room decorations.

WATCH IT FOR: Top tips on how to look good without blowing the budget. Great fashion DIY vlogs show you how to create something amazing by using craft supplies and charity shop finds

to update and upcycle your wardrobe. You'll learn how to make lots of different fashion, stationery and décor items, plus you get to feel super creative!

HOW TO: Just get hands-on with anything that can be created with supplies from a craft store. If you've got a passion for arts and crafts and a love for clothes, this is the perfect video upload for you to share your skills with the world.

7

THE HAUL

>>>>>>>>>>>>>>>

WHAT IS IT: The haul video is an amazingly popular trend where vloggers show off all the things they've bought during a shopping spree. Some focus on specific shops, some focus on times of year (back to school, holidays, summer) and some are just big splurges.

WATCH IT FOR: Top tips on where to pick up new outfit ideas, keep up with the trends and see what's in the shops without having to do all the legwork yourself. Follow a haul-er whose personal style you love and you'll most likely love their picks too!

HOW TO: Haul videos are usually chatty and informal, and the 'real' aspect of these videos is what makes them so enjoyable to watch. The ideal haul vlog should be both informative and enthusiastic. The format of a haul is to pull out new products one-by-one and talk about:
• Where you got them.
• Why you got them.
• How to wear them.
• How much they cost.

THE SHOP SPECIFIC HAUL

THE HOLIDAY HAUL

THE BACK TO SCHOOL HAUL

THE TRY-ON HAUL

THE LOOKBOOK

>>>>>>>>>>>>>>>

WHAT IS IT: A live action photo shoot, where the vlogger models different outfits they have put together. Lookbooks show the upcoming trends for each season or month.

WATCH IT FOR: Spotting new trends at the start of a season, and for inspiration on how to put an outfit together.

HOW TO: Lookbooks are very stylised videos, and usually have a soundtrack but no voiceover. Show off your looks in different poses with close-ups of details on the clothes and your make-up look. Ask a friend to film you, and make sure to include details of each item in the description box.

PLAN YOUR SEASONAL LOOKBOOK

CHOOSE A SEASON:

SPRING   SUMMER   AUTUMN   WINTER

Use the space below to plan the outfits you'll show. Add details such as where they're from, how much they cost, and other ways you'd wear them.

TOP 10 FASHION VLOGGERS

Whether you need a new look for a night out, are in desperate need of styling tips or simply stuck in a fashion rut, you can always depend on the fashion vloggers for some style inspiration. Check out the top YouTubers you should subscribe to, whether you're looking for hauls, how-tos, or just some fashion fun.

10. INTHEFROW

+534K

>>>>>>>>>>>>>>>

NAME: Victoria Magrath
ON YOUTUBE SINCE: November 2012
WATCH HER FOR: Her colourful locks and impeccable taste.

With a PhD in mobile fashion app design and a stint as a fashion lecturer, it's safe to say Victoria from Inthefrow knows what she's talking about when it comes to style. Her channel is filled with shopping hauls, shoe collections, monthly favourites and beauty get-the-looks. Warning: you may experience serious style envy – whether it's her killer wardrobe, cool hair, massive make-up collection or glamorous vacations – we just want to be her.

> Favourite brands:
> Jeffery Campbell, Zara,
> H&M and Topshop.

9. SHIRLEY B. ENIANG

+721K

>>>>>>>>>>>>>>

NAME: Shirley B. Eniang
ON YOUTUBE SINCE: December 2008
WATCH HER FOR: Inspirational and easy-to-follow fashion advice, from haul videos to hair tutorials.

London-based Shirley is the queen of simple style. Her gorgeous channel is full of crisp white backgrounds, perfect editing and sophisticated style. Along with the impeccable outfits and inspirational lookbooks she specialises in, Shirley gives great tips on how to develop your own personal style, and her warm personality shines through in every video. It's no wonder her motto is to: "allow your true beauty to shine from within."

8. PATRICIA BRIGHT

>>>>>>>>>>>>>>>

NAME: Patricia Bright
ON YOUTUBE SINCE: February 2009
WATCH HER FOR: Innovative fashion and beauty videos and random life musings.

+990K

From accounting student to style queen, long gone are the days where Patricia Bright used to make whispered videos in the bathroom of her shared student house. With a considerable and loyal following, Patricia now loves to share her wardrobe secrets with the world. She's also well known for dispensing valuable advice to her viewers – from confidence tips to how-to tutorials; you're bound to pick up a trick or two.

7. MADDI BRAGG

>>>>>>>>>>>>>>>

1.3 MILLION

NAME: Maddi Bragg
ON YOUTUBE SINCE: April 2011
WATCH HER FOR: Cool, fashion forward content with an edgy vibe.

After joining YouTube at the age of 12, California girl Maddi Bragg has worked with major brands and quickly risen up the ranks to become one of YouTube's top teenage fashion gurus. Phew! Viewers have seen her style evolve from the sweet, shy tween with braces to one of the edgiest fashion vloggers on YouTube today. Her videos cover everything from cool lookbooks to back to school hauls, challenges and make-up tutorials. Plus, her Insta feed is to die for.

6. TESS CHRISTINE

>>>>>>>>>>>>>>

+2.1 MILLION

NAME: Tess Christine
ON YOUTUBE SINCE: April 2008
WATCH HER FOR: Get-the-look tutorials inspired by all your fave celebs, plus outfit inspo for all occasions, easy DIYs and seasonal styles.

Tess Christine is a fashion vlogger from Minnesota, who is best known for her awesome 'Get The Look: Celebspiration' videos. If you've ever wanted to know how to steal the style of your favourite stars, Tess is your go-to girl. She's recreated the looks of loads of celebs, from Kendall and Kylie to Gigi Hadid and the Pretty Little Liars. Her tutorials are super easy to follow, showing how to recreate red carpet and everyday hair, outfit and make-up looks for less.

5. CLOTHESENCOUNTERS

>>>>>>>>>>>>>>

+1.7 MILLION

NAME: Jenn Im
ON YOUTUBE SINCE: February 2010
WATCH HER FOR: Style musings, tutorials and lifestyle advice with a pinch of humour.

Fashion vlogger Jenn Im started her cleverly named channel clothesencounters, as a way to combine her loves of fashion and video editing, and it's definitely paid off. With her beautifully shot lookbooks, chic outfit diaries, hauls and how-to styling tips, it's become THE go-to channel for fashion and lifestyle advice on YouTube. Jenn treats her audience like old friends, messing around on camera and sharing intimate details of her life as well as fashion tips, and it's this sense of realness that her fans love most. Her honest reviews are a breath of fresh air and the easy-to-follow how-to styling videos are guaranteed to give you some outfit inspiration. With Jenn's infectious energy and passion for fashion, you can ensure the video-watching experience is always a fun one.

Jenn loves mixing and matching clothes, using high range items and thrifty pieces to create the perfect outfit.

"My main message for my channel is to wear whatever makes you feel good... Life is too short to wear something you don't like."

 FASHION

4. EVELINA

1.2 MILLION

>>>>>>>>>>>>

NAME: Evelina Barry

ON YOUTUBE SINCE: May 2008

WATCH HER FOR: An online fashion diary, where she shares styling tips, DIYs, visually stunning short films and everything in between.

Obsessed with everything fashion, Evelina shares her passion for styling and DIY projects on her channel. Here, you'll find stunning videography skills mixed with top-notch fashion sense, impressive DIY makes, hair and make-up tutorials, and styling videos to create runway looks on any budget. Evelina's goal is to make fashion accessible for everyone, taking inspiration from top trendsetters to create her own fabulous look, on a real girl's budget.

> Evelina would love to be a fashion editor for Vogue.

3. SAMANTHA MARIA

1.8 MILLION

>>>>>>>>>>>>

NAME: Samantha Maria

ON YOUTUBE SINCE: July 2009

WATCH HER FOR: Her unique, edgy style and intimate chats.

Samantha Maria is a fashion styling graduate turned designer (she recently launched her own label called Novem & Knight), so as you might expect, her fashion-based YouTube channel is pretty darn good. Sammi regularly treats her viewers to videos about her life and longstanding love of fashion. She showcases her cool street style in slickly shot lookbooks, and along with chatty hauls, beauty tutorials and monthly faves, she adds advice about self-confidence, friends and bad relationships. What more could you need?

> Samantha's top tip:
> "Create videos and a blog about something you would like to watch and read about yourself. I will sometimes ask myself such things as 'Would I want to watch that myself?' before I create a video."

2. MARZIA

+6.7 MILLION

>>>>>>>>>>>>>>

NAME: Marzia Bisognin

ON YOUTUBE SINCE: January 2012

WATCH HER FOR: Girly fashion inspiration with a sweet sprinkling of entertainment.

Marzia, aka CutiePieMarzia must be doing something right – her fashion-centred YouTube channel has managed to gain over 6 million subscribers in just four years! We put it down to her great sense of fashion, sweet personality and mixed-bag of creative content – from lookbooks and hauls to DIY videos, travel vlogs, recipes, make-up tutorials, monthly favourites, and cute cartoons featuring her pugs, Edgar and Maya. Oh, and it probably doesn't hurt that her boyfriend, PewDiePie, happens to be the biggest YouTuber in the world, either.

> Marzia calls her fans her "marzipans".

>> QUEEN OF THEM HAUL!

1. BETHANY MOTA

>>>>>>>>>>>>>>>

NAME: Bethany Noel Mota
BORN: 7 November 1992
FIND HER AT: youtube.com/MacBarbie07
ON YOUTUBE SINCE: June 2009
WATCH HER FOR: Colourful, upbeat videos on everything from routines and room tours to outfit ideas, DIY tricks and, of course, her signature hauls.

Bethany Mota has been the go-to channel for fashion hauls and style tips since the early days of YouTube. In 2009, a shy 13-year-old Bethany began making videos to share her passion for fashion and beauty, as well as to fend off loneliness after being bullied online. She was one of the first YouTubers to adopt the haul video, and her channel has since evolved to include tutorials of all kinds, DIY tips and life advice. Her life has changed quite a bit since then, too – with over 10 million subscribers she is now one of the most successful YouTube stars in the world. In between her amazing tutorials and Motavator meet-and-greets, Bethany has turned her hand to music, interviewed President Obama, made it to the finals of 'Dancing with the Stars' and even released her own clothing line for Aéropostale! Despite all this, Bethany says she'll never give up making YouTube videos. "YouTube is where it started for me, and that's the one place that I can constantly be creative," she says. Thank goodness for that.

+10.3 MILLION

"I'll make videos until I'm 60 if you guys want to watch them!"

MOST WATCHED VIDEO: Her 'Healthy Back to School Lunches!' video has over 15 million views!

Beth calls her fans Motavators, and considers having millions of fans to be like having millions of friends. "That's why the relationship with a YouTube creator and their audience is so strong and powerful: it's the same as a friendship."

TIP TO GET TO THE TOP:

"Never put yourself in a box."

Just because you started out doing one thing on YouTube doesn't mean you have to limit yourself. Like Beth, you can experiment and try different things on your channel, whether it's beauty, fashion or DIY.

FASHION

STYLE GOALS!

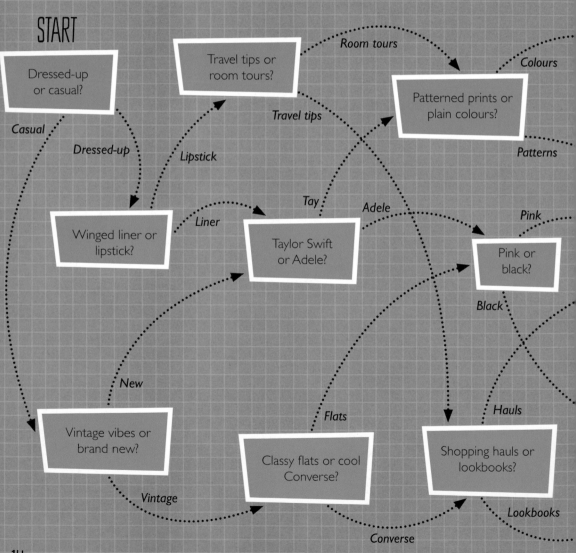

START

Dressed-up or casual?

Travel tips or room tours?

Room tours

Colours

Patterned prints or plain colours?

Casual

Dressed-up

Travel tips

Patterns

Lipstick

Winged liner or lipstick?

Liner

Tay

Adele

Pink

Taylor Swift or Adele?

Pink or black?

Black

New

Vintage vibes or brand new?

Flats

Classy flats or cool Converse?

Hauls

Shopping hauls or lookbooks?

Vintage

Converse

Lookbooks

Which of these fashion vloggers' videos should you be watching? They might not have as many subs (yet!) as some of the better-known stars but they're already total style gurus. Work your way across the flowchart, picking the choices that suit you best to discover which YouTuber shares your fashion sense.

Girly

Girly or edgy?

Edgy

Ted Baker

Primark or Ted Baker?

Primark

Hat

Statement sunglasses or stylish hat?

Sunglasses

FREDDY MY LOVE

If you're into all things pink and girly, you're going to LOVE Freddy My Love. Like Freddy, your style is sweet and pretty, and you definitely appreciate the finer things in life. Freddy should be your go-to guru for beauty tutorials, 'Get Ready With Me' videos and some serious life goals!

BECCA ROSE

Bubbly London girl Becca Rose has some serious style – check out her channel for classy, feminine glamour with a 60s vibe. Like Becca, you can haul till you fall. Becca's vids are full of fashion, beauty and home hauls, and since she uploads new videos every Monday, Wednesday and Friday you'll have a never-ending supply of shopping inspo.

SUNBEAMSJESS

Fashion YouTuber sunbeamsjess is the definition of cool. If you prefer your look with a little more edge, Jess is the vlogger for you. Check out her channel for beautifully shot lookbooks and laid-back outfit inspiration – think statement sunglasses, oversized denim, vintage sportswear, layered accessories and 90s vibes.

#LIFEINSPO

Lifestyle vloggers make videos about all the normal things you'd chat about with your friends – travel, relationships, fashion, food and family – the only difference is the whole world's watching them! We love to check in for their regular updates, and because let's face it, these YouTube gurus are #goals. Here are just some of the ways they let us into their lives.

WHAT MAKES A LIFESTYLE VLOGGER?

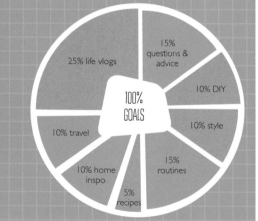

15% questions & advice
25% life vlogs
10% DIY
100% GOALS
10% style
10% travel
15% routines
10% home inspo
5% recipes

DID YOU KNOW? Charles Trippy from the CTFxC channel holds the Guinness World Record for filming and uploading his daily vlogs to YouTube without skipping a single day. As of 19 December 2016, he's up to 2,933 consecutive videos!

DAILY VLOGS
>>>>>>>>>>>>

WHAT IS IT: Some vloggers are brave enough to upload footage from their lives every single day, giving viewers a unique insight into everything they get up to, from hanging out with friends to shopping trips, restaurant outings, travel diaries and quality time with family.

WATCH IT FOR: An easy way to get to know the stars of the Internet on a more personal level. They let us into their homes, share the fun times in their lives, their opinions and emotions with us and as a result come to feel like close friends. It's like tuning into reality TV, except much more real and relatable than watching the Kardashians!

HOW TO: If you prefer to keep your life private, then daily vlogging is not for you! These vloggers have a passion to record and document their lives everyday, so if you want to give it a go, commitment is what you'll truly need. Uploading and editing vlogs to meet a daily deadline can be a lot of work and many struggle to keep it up. CaseyNeistat is the king of daily vlogging, so check out his channel if you want some inspiration.

TOP TIPS

• Film your day! If something fun is happening, make sure to record it. You don't need a fancy camera — part of the appeal of lifestyle vlogs is their realness. Just make sure the camera isn't too shaky.
• Get confident. Pretend you're chatting to a friend when you talk to the camera and you'll soon find your vlogs flow naturally.

• Edit! Cut your footage into a montage of the day's highlights.
• Get permission. People you know may not want to be filmed so respect their decision.
• Stay safe! Remember anyone on the web can watch your videos so don't film anything illegal or personal. Don't mention where you go to school or work and keep your address secret.

VLOGMAS

>>>>>>>

WHAT IS IT: December means only one thing in the vlogging calendar: Vlogmas! Every year, a variety of vloggers take on the popular challenge to upload a festive vlog every day in the run up to Christmas — it's like an amazing video advent calendar!

WATCH IT FOR: A daily insight into the things your fave YouTubers get up to during the busiest season of the year. With all the Christmas parties, vlogger events and festive fun, Vlogmas is bound to be extra exciting. Our festive faves are Zoella, Tanya Burr, Fleur DeForce, Sprinkleofglitter and ThatcherJoe, who usually give it a go each year.

HOW TO: It's just like filming a daily vlog, but with more festive footage! Vlogmas is a good way to try out daily vlogging when you have more time over the Christmas holidays without committing to it for the rest of the year. It's also heaps of fun: vloggers say it encourages them to do more exciting things with their days so they always have something to film! As well as filming their daily antics, other popular Vlogmas vids are:

- Decoration DIYs
- Baking seasonal treats
- Festive make-up
- Christmas shopping
- Gift guides
- Christmassy hauls

FUN FACT! Ingrid Nilsen was actually the creator of Vlogmas in 2011! I know, we thought it had been a thing since forever ago too.

THE ROOM TOUR

>>>>>>>>>>>>>

WHAT IS IT: The room tour tag is often a highly requested video, where a vlogger gives their viewers a virtual tour around their room or even their entire house.

WATCH IT FOR: Having a bit of a nosey round someone else's digs, let's be honest. As well as getting a sneaky peek at someone else's place, room tours are a great way to get ideas on how to decorate, as well as organisation inspo, storage tips and massive motivation to tidy your own room. Seriously, who keeps their room that tidy?

HOW TO: In these videos, vloggers will usually give a quick intro before giving a 360-degree tour of their room, pointing out items as they go. They'll tell the story behind special items, let us know where they got things from, and of course, give a glimpse into their wardrobes (which can sometimes be a video in itself).

17

THE MORNING ROUTINE

> > > > > > > > > > > > > > >

WHAT IS IT: YouTube is full of 'routine' videos – night routines, school routines, routines for every season – but the morning routine video is the most popular of them all. In these videos vloggers share how they usually like to start their day, filming their each and every move, from the alarm going off to picking out the perfect outfit, checking social media, making breakfast and heading out the door.

WATCH IT FOR: A peek into the YouTubers' lives beyond their usual setting. We get to see what they like to eat, how they get ready and even what kind of shampoo they use. While you're still hitting the snooze button, it seems they've already got up, been for a run, made a healthy breakfast, put together a flawless outfit and tweeted to their thousands of fans!

HOW TO: You'll need someone else to film you. The most popular routine videos are professionally edited, with a voiceover narrating what they're doing at every step, so it's definitely a chance to put your editing skills to the test. If you fancy trying something a little less perfect, 'My REAL Routine' videos show the reality of most people's daily routines, while there are also fun spoofs of the popular tag where the routine doesn't quite go to plan…

THE Q&A

> > > > > > > > > > > > > > >

WHAT IS IT: Basically, it's exactly what it sounds like. Vloggers often get a lot of questions from fans – part of the problem with putting your life on the Internet is that people always want to know more! In these chatty videos, they sit-down in front of the camera to try and answer some of the questions, which range from things like 'What's your favourite pizza topping?' to more serious questions.

WATCH IT FOR: Getting to know your faves a bit better and finding out the answers to those burning questions you've been dying to ask. Vloggers usually open up a fair bit in Q&A videos and they're great for building relationships and engaging with fans.

HOW TO: Q&As are simple, so vloggers love to film them when they don't have much time or are all out of ideas! The questions are usually taken from the comments section on YouTube or other social media such as Twitter. When it comes to filming, the more thought you put into your answers, the better. Display a screenshot of each question on screen and give shout-outs of each person's username. The beauty of this video is that you can pick whichever questions you feel comfortable answering, and it can be used for literally any kind of channel!

WATCH:

'Youtubers Morning Routine' - ThatcherJoe

IF YOU DON'T HAVE ANY QUESTIONS YET, SIMPLY LOOK AT THE NEXT PAGE!

THE QUESTIONS NOBODY ASKS TAG!

> >

Are you ready to Q and slay? This popular tag is a fun alternative to the normal Q&A, where you answer '50 Questions Nobody Asks'. This would make for a great first YouTube video, or you could just have fun answering the questions with friends!

- Do you sleep with your closet doors open or closed?

- Do you sleep with your sheets tucked in or out?

- Do you like to use post-it notes?

- Do you have freckles?

- Would you rather be attacked by a big bear or a swarm of bees?

- What is your favourite kind of sandwich?

- Do you always smile for pictures?

- What is your biggest pet peeve?

- Have you ever peed in the woods?

- Do you ever dance even if there's no music playing?

- Do you chew your pens and pencils?

- What size is your bed?

- Are you stubborn?

- Do you ever watch soap operas?

- Are you afraid of heights?

- Do you sing in the car or the shower?

- Do you believe in ghosts?

- Do you wear slippers?

- What do you drink with dinner?

- What do you dip a chicken nugget in?

- What is your favourite food?

- What movie could you watch over and over and still love?

- Who is the last person you kissed?

- Were you ever a boy/girl scout?

- Where would you bury hidden treasure if you had some?

- How many languages can you speak?

- What is the best thing to eat for breakfast?

- What is your usual bedtime?

WHO DO YOU TAG TO ANSWER THE QUESTIONS NEXT?

- Do you still watch cartoons?

- What's your least favourite movie?

TOP 10 LIFESTYLE VLOGGERS

We regularly turn to lifestyle vloggers for updates on their lives, style, routines, regimes and #lifeinspo, and end up learning so much about them that they really start to feel like friends. Here are some of our favourite lifestyle stars who are bound to entertain you – just by being themselves!

10. THE ANNA EDIT

>>>>>>>>>>>>>

NAME: Anna Gardner
ON YOUTUBE SINCE: April 2010
WATCH HER FOR: A mixed bag of beauty, style, food, life advice, weekly vlogs, wellness and fitness.

+399K

Veteran blogger Anna (previously known as ViviannaDoesMakeup) isn't new to the YT scene, but her current focus on lifestyle is something that has evolved and grown with her over the years. Anna shares anything and everything that she's currently into, including fashion favourites, fitness routines and delicious dinner ideas, as well as her on-point beauty advice. Her warm and witty personality shines in her twice-weekly YouTube videos, and we especially love it when Anna vlogs (complete with the occasional pop-in from hubby-to-be, Mark).

9. ESTÉE LALONDE

+1.1 MILLION

>>>>>>>>>>>>>

NAME: Estée Lalonde
ON YOUTUBE SINCE: March 2011
WATCH HER FOR: Entertaining vlogs and inspiring life insights, plus Reggie the dog, obvs.

Canadian born, London-based Estée has been regularly sharing make-up tips and peeks into her life with boyfriend, Aslan, and dog, Reggie, for over five years. You may have known her as Essie Button the beauty guru, but with the rebranding of her channel to her real name, she's now taking things to a new level of personal. With Estee's charming and approachable personality and her original content (plus loads of vlogs on second channel Everyday Estée), it's hard not to get hooked. With a lifestyle book in the works, several awards under her belt, a huge online following and the personality to boot, we can't wait to see what she's going to do next.

9. ASPYN + PARKER

+1.4 MILLION

>>>>>>>>>>>>>

NAME: Aspyn Ovard & Parker Ferris
ON YOUTUBE SINCE: January 2011
(Parker joined in 2014)
WATCH THEM FOR: Regular vlogs following the love story and daily lives of one of YouTube's cutest young couples.

While Aspyn Ovard is best known for her own super successful beauty and lifestyle channel, it's her more personal channel with hubby Parker that we just can't get enough of. The high school sweethearts were married young at the ages of 19 and 20 and now make YouTube videos full-time, documenting their everyday lives and adventures as one of YouTube's most adorable couples. From their engagement in Greece to their entire wedding process and trips all over the world, this pair lets us in on every step of their exciting lives.

7. FLEUR DEFORCE

>>>>>>>>>>>>>>

+1.4 MILLION

NAME: Fleur Bell

ON YOUTUBE SINCE: September 2009

WATCH HER FOR: A mix of beauty, hauls, home, life vlogs, favourite things and even wedding inspo – basically something for everyone.

> Fleur picked up tips on how to run a successful channel by watching her fave YouTubers for a year before posting her own content.

If Fleur DeForce wasn't so darn lovely, we'd probably hate her. She has over a million subscribers on YouTube, two bestselling books, all the beauty products you could ever wish for, a handsome hubby, gorgeous house, heaps of awards and is basically an all-round inspiration; proving that hard work really does pay off. She shares a glimpse into the glam life on her second channel FleurDeVlog, where you can watch as she launches beauty lines and books, travels around the world and slays every day. On her main channel, Fleur delivers make-up tutorials and lifestyle advice like she's talking to an old friend, as well as sharing monthly favourites, hauls, home décor tips and product reviews. We don't know how she has time for it all but one thing's for sure – Fleur is a force to be reckoned with.

> **WATCH:** 'Our Wedding Day'. Fleur married her husband Mike back in 2013, and her wedding video has got to be the most perf things we've ever seen.

6. SACCONEJOLYS

>>>>>>>>>>>>>>

+1.7 MILLION

NAME: Anna and Jonathan Saccone-Joly

ON YOUTUBE SINCE: December 2009

WATCH THEM FOR: Daily family vlogs for your reality show fix (plus Emilia and Eduardo are the absolute cutest).

The SACCONEJOLYs: Anna, Jonathan, and little ones Emilia and Eduardo (plus their six Maltese dogs), are a family of Irish vloggers living in London who welcome you to watch them live their lives together every day. What makes this online family so real is that they share pretty much everything that goes on in their lives, from major moments like a marriage proposal and their beautiful wedding, to the births of both of their children and all of the highs and lows of everyday life.

5. POINTLESSBLOGVLOGS

>>>>>>>>>>>>>>

+3.7 MILLION

NAME: Alfie Deyes

ON YOUTUBE SINCE: March 2010

WATCH HIM FOR: Wishing we were an extended member of the Deyes Sugg family, plus lots of laughs and general silliness.

PointlessBlogVlogs is Alfie Deyes' vlogging channel where he keeps his millions of fans in the loop on everything he's been up to. Now, normally watching somebody else's every move online might be a bit boring (and also creepy), but Alfie's life is literally LOADS of fun. The chirpy Brighton boy shares access to all his silly antics, business meetings, cool conventions and of course life in the Zalfie pad with gf Zoella, adorable pup Nala and their many YouTuber mates. It's clear to see that Alfie loves to vlog and each video features the cheeky spirit, honest and loveable personality he's known for. Fair warning – you may fall a little bit in love with him.

21

4. MEREDITH FOSTER

>>>>>>>>>>>>>

+4.7 MILLION

NAME: Meredith Foster
ON YOUTUBE SINCE: August 2009
WATCH HER FOR: All round life inspo: beauty, fashion, fitness, hair and home how-tos, daily routines and monthly must-haves.

Meredith Foster has amassed a following of over 4 million subscribers since launching her lifestyle, fashion and beauty channel, and with her vibrant personality and flawless videos it's not hard to see why. Her channel is all about being confident in your own skin and she's a big believer that beauty comes from within. The fashion sensation provides upbeat tutorials, DIY hacks, outfit ideas and fun things to do with your friends that reflect her low maintenance style and big personality.

Meredith has a twin brother, Michael, who has appeared in some of her vlogs.

3. SHAYTARDS

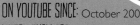

+4.8 MILLION

NAME: Shay Carl and Colette Butler
ON YOUTUBE SINCE: October 2008
WATCH THEM FOR: A never-ending supply of daily vlogs – this lot have been sharing their lives online for over seven years!

Probably the most successful vlogging family of all are the SHAYTARDS - the all-American family with five children and over 4 million subscribers. These guys basically invented the idea of family vlogging, making millions by simply living their lives and pressing record, with their channel motto: "If life's worth living then it's worth recording!". It's not hard to see why they've become so successful: they're the ultimate happy family, always laughing and having fun together and their positivity is infectious! Once you've watched one vlog it's hard to stop – we've watched so many it actually feels like we have a second family.

The SHAYTARDS all have nicknames! The five children are 'Sontard', 'Princesstard', 'Babytard', 'Rocktard' and 'Brotard', along with 'Mommytard' and dad 'Shaytard'.

2. MYLIFEASEVA

>>>>>>>>>>>>>

NAME: Eva Gutowski
ON YOUTUBE SINCE: July 2011
WATCH HER FOR: A colourful channel packed with Eva's fave things and fun personality; with outfit ideas, life tips, Tumblr-inspired DIYs and comedy skits.

+7.4 MILLION

MyLifeAsEva aka Eva Gutowski is literally goals. Over the past three years her online fan base has rocketed, making hers one of the fastest growing channels on YouTube. She slays the editing game with her colourful videos and creative intros, but the best thing about Eva is that she's 100% real and relatable. She isn't afraid to be silly in front of the camera and her comedy sketches, facial expressions and realistic routine videos are hilarious. Eva's also a role model and friend to her millions of fans, guiding them through the tough teen years and beyond with her 'How to Survive High School' series, tips to make friends, affordable outfit ideas and things to do for fun. If you're not an #evanator yet, you should be.

WATCH: Eva's original music video, 'Literally My Life'. The song has over 25 million views and will get stuck in your head for DAYS.

>> #GOALS

1. ZOELLA

>>>>>>>>>>>>>

NAME: Zoë Elizabeth Sugg

BORN: 28 March 1990

FIND HER AT: youtube.com/zoella280390 & /MoreZoella

ON YOUTUBE SINCE: February 2007

WATCH HER FOR: Monthly faves, chatty advice, beauty tutorials, Q&As, fashion inspo, day-in-the-life vlogs, how-tos, hauls, silly collabs and all the LOLs.

+11.4 MILLION

Who else could we have at #1 but Queen of YouTube, Zoella! Zoë is still an unstoppable force on YouTube, taking over the beauty, fashion and lifestyle world, casually winning countless awards and racking up over 11 million subscribers and 880 million video views! She's also seamlessly made the leap from online idol to offline superstar with two chart-topping books, a best-selling beauty range and an actual waxwork tribute at Madame Tussauds. We're betting that even your parents know who she is! Even though we might be a tiny bit jealous, all this success couldn't go to a nicer girl. With her great advice, loyal nature and positive attitude towards life, Zoella is like the big sister you've always dreamed of having. In her main channel videos, Zoë shares all the things she loves, items she's bought, advice and tips about make-up, hair, fashion and life. Her vlogging channel, MoreZoella, gives us all a glimpse into the dream life of a superstar vlogger, complete with conventions, fun road trips, Brighton beach walks, fan meet-ups, brothers, boyfriends, laughter, best friends and one adorable pug. Oh Zoë, please be our BFF!

> "BE THE BEST VERSION OF YOU."

> "DO WHAT YOU WANT TO DO AND DO IT FOR YOU."

Zoë was named as one of the Most Inspirational Women of the Decade in 2015 by Grazia magazine.

ONES TO WATCH: The up-and-coming stars to add to your subscription box.

EVE BENNETT Get unbeli-EVE-able exam advice, revision tips and faves from this rising star, who's gained support from the likes of Gabriella Lindley and Zoella.

MEG SAYS One of the nicest girls on YT, Meg delivers chatty videos, vlogs, tutorials and Q&As that are positive and inspirational. Plus, her voice is super soothing.

THE MICHALAKS Cute couple The Michalaks and even cuter baby, Grayson, upload amazingly edited weekly vlogs that could almost count as mini movies.

A-Z OF ZOELLA

A IS FOR ANXIETY
Zoella is super honest about her anxiety, bravely sharing her helpful tips and experiences with panic attacks in her videos. She's done a lot to get the issue of mental health out in the open, representing the charity MIND and even starting her own campaign – #DontPanicButton.

B IS FOR BRIGHTON
Head to Zoë's hometown Brighton and you might just catch her sipping hot chocolate in a cute café or strolling along the seafront pier.

C IS FOR COLLABS
From yoga moves with Caspar to awful accents with Marcus and the boyfriend tag with Tyler, Zoë's collabs are always hilarious.

DID YOU KNOW? Zoë's most viewed video is her '7 Second Challenge' collab with Miranda Sings.

D IS FOR DISNEY
If you're a Zoella fan you'll already know how much she loves all things Disney. Think of all the Disney film and pizza nights we could have if we were friends!

E IS FOR EMOTIONS
Zoë has said that the sun makes her feel instantly happy, while rain makes her instantly sad.

F IS FOR FRIENDS
As well as being Internet best friend to 11m subscribers, Zoë has loads of great mates IRL. Her closest circle includes other amazing vloggers like Tanya, Louise, Gabby, Jim and new BFF Mark Ferris.

G IS FOR GOALS
She is ALL of the goals… #hairgoals #familygoals #housegoals #bfgoals #petgoals #squadgoals #lifegoals.

H IS FOR HARRY POTTER
Not only is Zoë a huge Harry Potter fan, but she even got to be an extra in both the first and second films!

Aladdin is her fave Disney film.

I IS FOR INSPIRATION
Zoë is a total girl boss and inspo for us all. She's turned blogging in her bedroom into a successful business and brand with books, beauty products and fans all over the world. #proud

J IS FOR JOE SUGGS
Aka the best brother ever! Can we share him?

K IS FOR KEEPIN' IT REAL
Even though she's loaded we love the fact that Zoë still shops on the high street and enjoys a good old Primark haul as much as the rest of us.

L IS FOR LOUISE
Sprinkleofglitter + Zoella = the ultimate BFF love story.
Chummies for life

M IS FOR MONTHLY FAVOURITES
Zoë's monthly fave videos are a must-watch. She lets us in on everything she's loved that month, from beauty bits to clothes and music, and we always want ALL of it.

N IS FOR NOVELS

Zoë's two novels, 'Girl Online' and 'Girl Online: On Tour', both became bestsellers in the space of no time at all. We're keeping all fingers crossed for a third.

O IS FOR OUTFITS

We're absolutely obsessed with Zoë's style, whether she's rocking pretty dresses, cosy knits or the cutest PJs. This girl knows how to put together the perfect outfit for any occasion.

P IS FOR PETS

Zoë is mother to two little guinea pigs, Pippin and Percy, and the world's most adorable pug, Nala.

Q IS FOR QUEEN

She's the undisputed Queen of the Internet – long may she reign and slay!

R IS FOR ROLE MODEL

We think it's great that someone with as much influence as Zoë uses her power to make the world a better place. Whether she's teaching body confidence or raising awareness for important issues, Zoë inspires us all to be more positive and happy.

S IS FOR SUBSCRIBERS

With 11 million subs on her main channel, and 4 million on her second, Zoë is one of the world's most subscribed-to vloggers, and that number is still rising every day.

T IS FOR TUTORIALS

Whether she's showing us an everyday make-up look or teaching us how to do her messy bun, Zoë's tutorials are always on-point and easy to follow.

U IS FOR UPLOADS

Zoë has uploaded over 300 videos on her main channel alone!

V IS FOR VLOGMAS

It's no secret that Zoë gets super excited about Christmas. WE get excited because Christmas means Vlogmas. 24 days of seeing Zoë's face everyday? YAAAAS.

W IS FOR WEIRDO

Zoë is not afraid to be who she is, and she is a TOTAL weirdo. We wouldn't have it any other way!

X IS FOR X-FACTOR

Ok so maybe not, but if she was on the show she'd defo win. Have you HEARD her sing? Girl's got talent.

Y IS FOR YES

Zoë is a firm believer in taking every opportunity life offers you. As she says, "saying yes to one small thing can lead to a whole other world of opportunities… It all starts at the word yes!".

Z IS FOR ZALFIE

Vlogging power-couple Alfie and Zoella are the ultimate in relationship goals, giving us all of the feels since 2013. And to think it all started with a tweet…

WATCH: 'The long awaited (real) boyfriend tag video'.

LIFESTYLE LOTTO You Tube

Ever wish you could live like a top vlogger? Get some serious life inspo of your own with these challenges to help you look like a YouTuber, live like a YouTuber and feel like a YouTuber!

1 MAKE A LIST of all the things you've been loving this month (you could even turn this into a 'Monthly Favourites' vid!).

2 MAKE A COLLAGE of old photos so you can look back at all the lovely memories you've made.

3 CUDDLE UP with a cute pet and take a selfie together!

4 GET HEALTHY and make a nutritious treat and get some exercise! You could even make a workout vid!

5 COME UP WITH three awesome outfits that fit the season you're in and take some snaps outdoors to star in your own fashion photo shoot.

6 ASK A FRIEND or sibling to collab with you to complete a challenge tag. Take it turns to ask each other questions from 'The Best Friend Tag' or 'The Sibling Tag.'

7 TAKE A FUN TRIP with friends and film the whole day, vlogger-style!

8 USE YOUTUBE VIDEOS as inspo to make a cute DIY decoration for your room to make it look picture perfect, ready for any room tour.

9 HAVE A SLEEPOVER with your BFF. Cosy up with blankets, hot chocolate and your favourite film.

10 USE A SUNDAY MORNING to nail your dream morning routine – set the alarm for your ideal wake up time, make your favourite breakfast, pick out the perf outfit – whatever you fancy!

11 COMPLETE A CHILLED-OUT night routine to relax after a hard day. Treat yourself to a face mask (there are loads of easy-to-make mask tutorials on YouTube), a nice bath or a good book.

12 BAKE SOME CUPCAKES or your favourite tasty treat. Yum!

COLOUR IN EACH SQUARE AS YOU COMPLETE EACH LIFESTYLE VLOGGER EXPERIENCE.

1	2	3	4
5	6	7	8
9	10	11	12

MUSIC MAKERS

WHAT MAKES A MUSIC YOUTUBER?

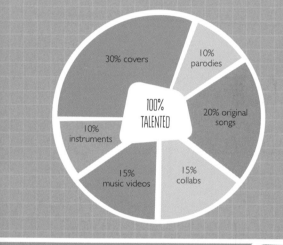

30% covers
10% parodies
100% TALENTED
20% original songs
10% instruments
15% music videos
15% collabs

YouTube is now the most popular source of on-demand music for young people today. You can find everything from the world's biggest artists to undiscovered talent, music of all genres, instruments of all kinds, hilarious parodies and cool covers. YouTube has become so important in today's music industry that it's actually changing the game – the Billboard music charts now count YouTube views when calculating the top songs list!

It's also changing the way that new talent is discovered. Music videos from the biggest pop stars get millions of views, but they're not the only ones racking up the hits (literally). Lots of talented musicians have gone from YouTube to the top of the charts by using the site as a springboard to widespread fame and fortune.

THE BIEBS

> > > > > > > > > > > > > > >

The most famous example of all YouTuber-turned-stars is of course, Justin Bieber. Whether you love him or hate him, you can't deny Bieber's huge success – so huge in fact, that many people aren't aware he started out on a little old site called YouTube. A true overnight success story, Justin went from being a young, untrained singer whose mother posted clips of him singing in his living room, to a budding star with a big-time record deal, all because his current manager Scooter Braun spotted a video of him on the site one night. We don't need to tell you more about his success story ('sorry'), but with an estimated $55 million in earnings last year, we're pretty sure Biebs isn't regretting sharing those YT videos right now.

Justin's VEVO channel is now the most subscribed to music channel on YouTube, with over 26 million subs. Check out his original channel kidrauhl to see baby Biebs' first videos! Bless.

PSY

>>>>>>>>>>>>>

South Korean singer-songwriter PSY became an international sensation with the quirky breakout hit 'Gangnam Style'. PSY has since got a record deal after Scooter Braun (this guy again!) flew the singer over to the U.S. after seeing the video. 'Gangnam Style' now has over 2.7 billion views and is the most-watched video in YouTube history. The vid actually BROKE YouTube's view counter, since the programmers never imagined a video would ever get that many views!

5SOS

>>>>>>>>>>>>>

Aussie band 5SOS might not even be a big deal if not for YouTube. Their journey began in 2011 after the boys met at school and started posting videos of themselves playing acoustic covers of pop and rock songs on YouTube. After building a local fan base, they rose to international fame when One D took notice and invited them on their 'Take Me Home' tour.

BOYCE AVENUE

>>>>>>>>>>>>>

Boyce Avenue started uploading their cover videos over nine years ago and now have over 2.8 billion views on their channel. Thanks to their early YT success they're still happily doing their own thang and hold the Guinness World Record for the 'Biggest Independent Band On The Planet On YouTube'!

THE WEEKND

>>>>>>>>>>>>>

Who knew The Weeknd launched his career online? He started posting YouTube videos of R&B tracks back in 2010 and they quickly went viral.

CONOR MAYNARD

>>>>>>>>>>>>>

Conor started posting covers on YT, gained loads of online fans and then really came to attention after American singer Ne-Yo watched a cover version of his track 'Beautiful Monster'. Soon after, Ne-Yo became Maynard's mentor.

DID YOU KNOW?

Biebs has since helped other YT artists get their big breaks too. Whatta hero…

MADISON BEER Mr Biebs spotted teen singer Madison and tweeted a link to a video of her singing. She trended worldwide and later signed a record deal with the same label as Justin.

CARLY RAE JEPSEN Biebs is also responsible for the rise to fame of Carly Rae Jepsen. You probably know her insanely catchy song 'Call Me Maybe', but you might not know that it was only after Justin shared the video that she really hit the big time. His tweet sent his manager Scooter Braun to YouTube, where he viewed various videos of Jepsen's singing before signing her up.

THIS LITTLE LOT ALL HAVE SOCIAL MEDIA TO THANK FOR THEIR MUSICAL STARDOM, TOO!

CODY SIMPSON　　CHARLIE PUTH　　TORI KELLY

ALESSIA CARA　　HALSEY　　SHAWN MENDES

AUSTIN MAHONE

TOP 10 YOUTUBE MUSICIANS

With so many musicians on YouTube showcasing their stuff, it can be hard to know where to look to find great new music. Whether you're looking for rock music or pop music, parodies, original songs or classics with a twist, we've got you covered with our pick of the top talented musicians. Some of them even have more subs than Beyoncé!

10. DODDLEODDLE

+802K

>>>>>>>>>>>>>>>>

NAME: Dodie Clark
ON YOUTUBE SINCE: February 2011
WATCH HER FOR: Ukulele playing, quirky original songs and heartfelt lyrics.

With a lot of love from her loyal fans and fellow YouTubers alike, British YouTuber Dodie Clark is pretty much guaranteed greatness. Head to her channel and you will find quirky covers sung in perfect harmony with ukulele playing, collabs with ALL the talented peeps and original songs covering a range of subjects from messy flats to falling in love and having down days. Between her musical talent, candid vlogs and all-round adorableness, Dodie is most definitely one to watch.

WATCH: original song 'My Face'.

Dodie's first ever YT video was an original song called 'Rain', which she wrote when she was 15.

9. EMMABLACKERY

+1.2 MILLION

>>>>>>>>>>>>>>>>

NAME: Emma Blackery
ON YOUTUBE SINCE: May 2012
WATCH HER FOR: Catchy, relatable rock music and inspirational lyrics tackling some tough issues.

All-round entertainer Emma Blackery has always loved music, originally starting her channel as a way to upload her home-made song demos, covers and music videos. Since then, Emma has gained Internet fame with her hilarious sketches, no-nonsense advice series and healthy dose of sass and sarcasm, but now she's back on the music scene and better than ever. Her platform on YouTube, awesome pop punk musical style and strong vocals has lead to success in both the iTunes charts and in accomplishing her childhood dream of going on tour with Busted!

"I never would have imagined that my vlog would lead to me performing music."

8. TODRICKHALL

>>>>>>>>>>>>>>>>

NAME: Todrick Hall
ON YOUTUBE SINCE: May 2006
WATCH HIM FOR: Ridiculously creative mini musicals based on fairy tales but with modern themes.

+2.3 MILLION

Todrick Hall is a quadruple threat. He can sing, he can dance, he can act, and boy can he YouTube. He got his first shot at fame on 'American Idol', but after failing to make it to the finals, he did the best thing he could have done and started his own channel. His insane talent for pop culture parodies quickly went viral, sending him on the path to self-made fame and fortune. Todrick's elaborate videos make fairy tales come to life, with a mixture of comedy, Glee-style singing, dancing and a whole lot of Disney… what more could you want?!

"Keep dreaming and never let them tell you no."

7. MEGAN NICOLE

> > > > > > > > > > > > >

+3.8 MILLION

NAME: Megan Nicole Flores

ON YOUTUBE SINCE: December 2009

WATCH HER FOR: Amazing, soulful covers and catchy original tunes.

This super-talented YouTube star became interested in music at the age of 10 when her parents bought her a karaoke machine. She rose to fame in 2009 after she uploaded a cover of the Kings of Leon's 'Use Somebody' to YouTube. Her fan base quickly grew thanks to her amazing covers, friendly vlogs and superstar collabs. She's teamed up with other YouTube musicians including Conor Maynard and Lindsey Stirling. We love her original song 'Play It Cool', and we certainly think we look cool dancing to it.

5. THEPIANOGUYS

> > > > > > > > > > > > >

·5.2 MILLION

NAME: Steven Sharp Nelson, Jon Schmidt, Al van der Beek and Paul Anderson

ON YOUTUBE SINCE: March 2008

WATCH THEM FOR: Classical interpretations of modern hits, accompanied by impressive music videos.

ThePianoGuys are four normal dudes who combine their separate skills as a pianist, a cellist, a songwriter and a videographer to create one awesome super group. The group have become an Internet phenomenon with their clever and unusual takes on both classical and pop songs, creating mash-ups of the likes of Adele and Mozart and playing One D songs as you've never heard them before. ThePianoGuys appeal to all age groups and even if you're not usually a fan of classical music, their emotion-filled and epically-shot videos will take your breath away. From filming Frozen songs in a real icicle palace to playing piano on top of a thousand-foot cliff, these guys inspire with their stunning mix of music and film.

6. PAINT

> > > > > > > > > > >

+3.8 MILLION

NAME: Jon Cozart

ON YOUTUBE SINCE: December 2005

WATCH HIM FOR: A one-man a cappella show performing pop-culture parodies.

Jon Cozart shot to Internet fame with viral hits such as 'Harry Potter in 99 seconds' and the amazing 'After Ever After', which offers darker alternative endings to Disney classics. What's great is that Jon loves all the same things we love AND creates songs about them; from Disney movies to boy bands and even YouTube itself. His must-see musical comedy vids are not only hilarious but extremely well executed too. He is completely a one-man show: writing the songs, singing all the a cappella parts, recording and editing it together himself. Subscribe and prepare to be impressed!

> The average Paint music video takes about three months to make.

WATCH: 'Vine vs YouTube: The Song (ft. Thomas Sanders)'

4. MIRANDA SINGS

> > > > > > > > > > > > > >

+7.3 MILLION

NAME: Colleen Ballinger
ON YOUTUBE SINCE: January 2008
WATCH HER FOR: A hilarious musical treat and a master class in self-confidence.

Miranda Sings acts as both a music and comedy channel. The wannabe pop star was originally created by comedian Colleen Ballinger to poke fun at some of the people she'd seen trying to get famous on YouTube. Despite that, Miranda's proved to be an absolute hit – she's self-absorbed, gives terrible tutorials, sings badly and dances terribly, but we all love her anyway (if you don't, you're probably one of the haters). With over 7 million Mirfandas, a Netflix show, two tours and a book under her belt, we're thinking Adele better watch her back!

Miranda says: "Be who you wanna be, unless it's not good, then stop it."

3. LINDSEY STIRLING

> > > > > > > > > > > > > >

+8.7 MILLION

NAME: Lindsey Stirling
ON YOUTUBE SINCE: May 2007
WATCH HER FOR: Impressive music videos with dancing, cool costumes and serious violin skills.

In case you haven't already heard of her, Lindsey is one of the most talented musicians to come out of the YouTube world. Lindsey's unique blend of music, often called 'violin dubstep', proves that playing the violin can be seriously cool and she has the rare ability to make any song sound even better. She gives the violin treatment to all kinds of music; from film and video game scores to pop hits and collabs with everyone from John Legend to the Muppets! We can't stop watching her mesmerising music videos, which make us want to go out and get a violin, stat.

2. TROYE SIVAN

> > > > > > > > > > > > > >

+4.3 MILLION

NAME: Troye Sivan
ON YOUTUBE SINCE: October 2007
WATCH HIM FOR: Trendy synth-pop with deep lyrics and hidden meanings.

Troye's songwriting is largely autobiographical. He says, "I want everyone to find their own meaning in it and apply it to their own lives."

"Life is a dream right now"

Troye Sivan is officially 'a thing'. From YouTube sensation posting funny chats and covers from his room to fully-fledged musician with an official VEVO channel and worldwide tour, we've loved joining Troye on his journey to global domination. He's made it all look easy, but the truth is Troye's success is self-made and totally on his terms. Since starting his channel at just 12-years-old, Troye's written his own hits and built his own fan base – his first EP 'TRXYE' was promoted entirely by his fans on social media, who sent it to #1 in the iTunes charts in 58 countries. Troye's cool synth-pop songs mix his perf voice with progressive lyrics and he counts Taylor Swift and Adele among his supporters. Between major chart successes, winning prestigious awards and performing at music festivals, the YouTube uploads have been few and far between recently but we'll let him off – Troye's a busy boy these days.

"Let yourself be the person you've always secretly wanted to be."

>> TOP OF THE POPS

1. PTXOFFICIAL

>>>>>>>>>>>>>>>

NAME: Scott Hoying, Kevin Olusola, Kirstin Maldonado, Mitch Grassi and Avi Kaplan

FIND THEM AT: youtube.com/PTXofficial

ON YOUTUBE SINCE: September 2011

WATCH THEM FOR: Awesome a capella arrangements of all the greatest songs along with original material.

+12.2 MILLION

Pentatonix are a five-part a cappella powerhouse. After winning U.S. TV show 'The Sing-Off' in 2011, the group got a record deal but were soon dropped as the label didn't believe they could make it in the music industry. Not giving up, they turned to YouTube, where their incredible vocal harmonies have gained over 1 billion views. Pentatonix are now platinum-selling artists with sold-out tours, over 11 million subscribers and not one but two Grammy Awards, which is mega in the music world. They've also had a cameo in Pitch Perfect 2, a #1 album and they've performed with music legends like Stevie Wonder! They still find time for YouTube though. While they are best known for arranging a cappella versions of popular artists like Beyoncé and Lorde, they've recently started releasing more of their original material and we love it! Their own song 'Can't Sleep Love' is all kinds of catchy and the feel-good music video for 'Sing' features a ton of famous faces including Maisie Williams, Tyler Oakley and Anna Kendrick!

WATCH: 'No' (Meghan Trainor cover) – so good you will never need to listen to the original version again.

Their Grammy winning 'Daft Punk Medley' has more than 214 million views!

SUPERFRUIT

In 2013, Mitch and Scott started a separate YouTube channel called SUPERFRUIT, posting comedic vlogs, superstar collabs and a cappella mash-ups. The pair have proved to be immensely popular outside of Pentatonix for their BFF friendship and YouTuber collabs.

ONES TO WATCH:
The up-and-coming stars to add to your subscription box.

EBONY DAY MUSIC
When she's not hanging out with The Vamps, singing queen Ebony uploads amazing acoustic covers.

MUSICALBETHAN
Bethan Leadley uploads gorgeous songs and topical vlogs and has also bagged herself a job presenting on 4Music.

ANDREW HUANG
Super creative Andrew Huang makes music out of pans and any supplies he can find lying around, from pillows to telephones and even dental equipment.

FAMOUS NAMES

YouTube has created a whole new breed of celebrity, but what happens when the fame has come first? Mainstream mega-celebs themselves are now flocking to social media for even more exposure. Whether they want to promote their work or a cause close to their hearts, keep up with changing trends or show the real face behind the fame, there are more A-listers giving vlogging a go than ever before. Here are some of the best celeb channels to check out.

TOM FLETCHER

> > > > > > > > > > > > > >

The talented singer of McFly and McBusted fame uses his channel to share messages via vlogs with his equally awesome sister and fellow YouTuber, Carrie Hope Fletcher. In the videos, titled 'Dear Carrie', Tom shares his thoughts, things he's been up to and, of course, a bit of singing.

Tom also uploads with his wife Giovanna and cute sons Buzz and Buddy. The whole family provide heaps of adorable moments that will make you laugh and make you cry; from Tom's perfect wedding speech song to baby Buzz giggling at a dandelion and their amazingly creative baby announcements.

MAISIE WILLIAMS

> > > > > > > > > > > > > >

Given Maisie's love of social media it's no surprise she's joined the YouTube crew. The 'Game of Thrones' star is already good pals with Caspar Lee and has teamed up with the likes of Teens React and SUPERFRUIT, but now she's giving it a go solo. Though she'll only be updating occasionally, you can expect Q&A sessions, random musings, actual red carpet vlogging and plenty of Maisie's gloriously goofy personality.

According to Maisie, close pal Caspar is the main reason she decided to start a channel!

We challenge you to watch 'Buzz and the Dandelions' without cracking a smile!

SHAY MITCHELL

> >>>>>>>>>>>>

Just when we thought we couldn't love Shay Mitchell any more, we find out she has a YouTube channel AND she posts on the regs, yay! Subscribe for snippets of Shay's jet-set life, cool collabs and all the latest PLL goss. Plus, since Shay is always serving major style goals IRL, her channel is packed with outfit inspo, make-up must-haves and nail tutorials – her junk food inspired nails are our latest obsession.

AMY POEHLER

> >>>>>>>>>>>>

Better known for her roles in movies such as 'Mean Girls' and 'Inside Out', American actress Amy Poehler also has an awesome YouTube channel called Amy Poehler's Smart Girls. Amy launched the channel to celebrate the successes of young women around the world, showing that it's not only OK to be your weird and wonderful self – it's better when you are! Amy gives good advice on friends, jealousy and anxiety in the 'Ask Amy' series, and with smart life hacks showing everything from how to do eyeliner to how to change a tyre; Smart Girls shows you that girls really can do anything.

> The SmartGirls channel was co-created by producer Meredith Walker.

KARLIE KLOSS

> >>>>>>>>>>>>

Klossy is the channel of big-time supermodel/Taylor Swift bestie, Karlie Kloss. Karlie's slick vids show us what it's like behind the scenes on runway shows, music videos and glamorous shoots, including cameos from the likes of super-famous friends Taylor and Gigi. Plus, she proves that even supermodels can be seriously down-to-earth, sharing her honest advice on self-confidence and hard work and even uploading the odd home baking tutorial!

> "I've spent the majority of my life in front of a camera, but not MY camera, and that's where this is different. These are the things you didn't get to see before."

#SQUADGOALS

YouTube has created some of the most magical friendships ever known, all made possible by the power of the Internet. These are the squads we all dream of joining, the YouTube crews who keep giving us all of the #SquadGoals with every collab and group selfie they make.

Tyler Oakley & Troye Sivan

Whether they're filming the best collabs or picking up Teen Choice Awards together, we will never ever stop shipping Troyler.

THE BROMANCE

THE OTP

Caspar Lee & Joe Sugg

Jaspar were #roommategoals so we were heartbroken when we heard they were moving out. Luckily for us they now have twice the space so the pranks and bants can go on!

Zoella & Sprinkleofglitter

Best chums Louise and Zoë have shared their blooming friendship with the Internet world. These two are like peas in a pod and their best friend collabs, chummy chats and giggling fits never cease to make us smile.

THE CHUMMIES

Dan & Phil

Everybody knows that you 100% cannot have Dan without Phil. Dan's advice on how they made friends? "Stalk people until they become your friend."

THE DYNAMIC DUO

THE BEAUTY BESTIES

Lily Pebbles and The Anna Edit

These two bond over shopping trips and make-up chats and we love it.

Hannah Hart, Mamrie Hart & Grace Helbig

Once upon a time this YouTube trio collabed on a video together, and the three have been fast friends ever since. They've gone on a comedy tour together, made a movie and basically conquered the world.

THE HOLY TRINITY

Zoë Sugg, Alfie Deyes, Marcus Butler, Louise Pentland, Tanya Burr, Jim Chapman, Niomi Smart and Joe Sugg

This lot are the British YouTube super crew, known to many as the definition of 'YouTubers'. They spend loads of time together online and off – always popping up in each other's videos, going on holiday and touring together, constantly supporting each other and giving us the ultimate in #squadgoals. We would love nothing more than to be adopted into their adorable little friendship-family.

THE ULTIMATE SQUAD

Smosh

Smosh's Ian and Anthony have been BFFs since they met at school, before YouTube was even born!

THE FOREVER FRIENDS

WHICH YOUTUBERS WOULD MAKE UP YOUR DREAM SQUAD?

1
2
3
4
5

YouTube BOOK BOOM

Yes, Team Internet have turned their talents to writing too, and with all the book tours and bestsellers, there's bound to be plenty more tomes to come. From lifestyle guides to memoirs and even graphic novels, there are all kinds of YouTuber offerings out there and many more coming soon to a shelf near you!

NOVELS & FICTION

ZOE SUGG: 'Girl Online' and 'Girl Online: On Tour'

Zoella has two best-selling, record-breaking books and we love them both! The novels tell the story of anonymous teen blogger Penny, who blogs about school dramas, boys, panic attacks and the pressures of growing up. There's no word on whether there will be a 'Girl Online 3', but we hope so – we need to know what Penny does next!

CARRIE HOPE FLETCHER: 'On The Other Side'

John Green was an author before he was a YouTuber! Check out his amazing Young Adult books including 'The Fault in Our Stars' and 'Paper Towns'.

ELLE AND BLAIR FOWLER: 'Beneath the Glitter'

OLI WHITE: 'Generation Next'

JOHN GREEN: 'The Fault in Our Stars'

EDUCATIONAL/SCIENCE

CHARLIE MCDONNELL: 'Fun Science'

Charlie McDonnell has written an exciting new science book based on his popular video series, 'Fun Science' and we're really looking forward to learning some sciencey stuff!

GRAPHIC NOVELS & CARTOONS

TOMSKA: 'Art is Dead'

SIMON TOFIELD: 'Simon's Cat'

JOE SUGG: 'Username: Evie'

Joe's first book 'Username: Evie' became the fastest-selling graphic novel since records began! The book was even nominated for Children's Book of the Year!

HEALTH & LIFESTYLE

MICHELLE PHAN: 'Make Up: Your Life Guide to Beauty, Style, and Success – Online and Off'

GRACE HELBIG: 'Grace & Style: The Art of Pretending You Have It'

Grace has a massive YouTube channel, films, a talk show and now TWO New York Times best-selling books. Both of her funny guides to life landed at the #1 slot in the first week of sales.

ACTIVITY BOOKS

STAMPY CAT: 'Stampy's Lovely Book'

ALFIE DEYES: 'The Pointless Book' and 'The Pointless Book 2'

MEMOIRS

I, JUSTINE: 'An Analog Memoir'

DAN AND PHIL: 'The Amazing Book Is Not on Fire'

TABINOF was both amazing and not on fire and an instant #1 New York Times bestseller. The pair have also taken the book on tour around the globe!

SELF-HELP & ADVICE

PEWDIEPIE: 'This Book Loves You'

MARCUS BUTLER: 'Hello Life!'

COOKBOOKS

ROSANNA PANSINO: 'The Nerdy Nummies Cookbook'

TANYA BURR: 'Tanya Bakes'

LET'S GET LITERARY

WHAT MAKES A BOOKTUBER?

100%
BOOK LOVERS

20% book hauls
10% bookshelf tours
10% book tags & collabs
10% recommends
10% enthusiastic
20% book chats
20% reviews

While some YouTubers are off writing books, others are busy reading, reviewing and uploading videos about them! From young adult fiction to literary classics and everything in between, these YouTubers have channels entirely dedicated to talking about books, spreading the joys of reading across the web. Welcome to the world of BookTube!

BOOK REVIEWS

>>>>>>>>>>>>

WHAT IS IT: An unbiased review about a recently read book. Vloggers discuss what they thought about the book and are honest about their book-related feels. Reviews are usually spoiler free, but should mention beforehand if they're going to give away any major plot points!

WATCH IT FOR: Finding out more about a book before buying. Reviewers talk about books in detail so you can get a good idea if it's something you'd like to read. They also encourage discussions in the comments section, so you can get recommendations and discuss the books you've already read with other fans!

HOW TO: The best book reviews are well thought out and concise. It might help to jot down the main points you want to discuss before making the video. Incorporate a brief plot synopsis, your thoughts about the book and be honest! Everyone has a different viewpoint, and others may find it useful to hear yours!

BOOK HAULS

>>>>>>>>>>>>>>

WHAT IS IT: Like a beauty haul but with books! BookTubers save up all the books they've read over a period of time and showcase them all at once in one big book haul, ranging from three books to over 50!

WATCH IT FOR: Finding great new books to read, seeing what's popular and keeping updated on all the upcoming releases. Find a BookTuber who has similar tastes to you and you'll discover some new favourite reads that you might not have heard of otherwise.

HOW TO: Firstly, be enthusiastic and show each book one by one. List all the relevant information about it – the book title, the author, what it's about (no spoilers!) and your first impressions of it. The amount of info you include will make it easier for other people to decide if they want to pick up the book too!

TIP: Making a video response to another BookTuber's review and linking to it in the comments adds to the discussion and is a great way to draw attention to your own channel!

BOOKSHELF TOURS

>>>>>>>>>>>>>>>>

WHAT IS IT: Other YouTubers give house tours and room tours, so it's only natural that BookTubers give us bookshelf tours! In these very popular videos, readers show us all the books they have on their beautifully organised shelves.

WATCH IT FOR: Bossing up your bookshelves. This is the place to get serious shelf inspo, with rows upon rows of pretty books. Side note: rainbow bookshelves are the best thing ever. Plus, bookshelf tours serve as a good introduction to a vlogger's reading taste and personality.

HOW TO: Talk viewers through your bookshelves shelf-by-shelf, showing each book individually and saying the title and author. These videos usually have a voiceover and some like to use it to showcase their creative editing skills. Generally, bookshelf tours are a bit longer than other videos since there are so many books to get through!

WATCH: 'The Lizzie Bennet Diaries.' If you enjoy modern-day adaptations of classics, you'll love 'The Lizzie Bennet Diaries'. This web series was produced by vlogbrothers' Hank Green and is based on Jane Austen's 'Pride and Prejudice' – updated for the Internet era!

MAKE FRIENDS: BookTube is one of the smaller YT communities, but it's one of the easiest places to make friends! It's a welcoming and interactive community because everybody shares a genuine love of books. There are lots of ways to get involved, with readathons, book tags, reading challenges, live shows, and so on.

BOOKTUBE TERMINOLOGY

Watch a few vids and you'll soon discover that book vloggers have their very own lingo! We've got you covered with the BookTube basics:

BOOKTUBER = a person dedicated to producing book-related content on YouTube.

TBR = to be read. Basically refers to any books that you want to read but haven't yet.

READATHON = a reading marathon. A set amount of time that you dedicate to reading at the same time as others across the Internet, making reading much more social and interactive!

BOOKTUBEATHON = a week of readathons hosted by popular YouTubers. The community joins together and has fun with various video and reading challenges and lots of prizes!

READING CHALLENGES = fun book-related challenges that spread across YT. e.g. bookshelf scavenger hunts and book tower challenges.

WRAP UP = short book reviews. Usually done at the end of the month, wrap ups feature short summaries about all the books read that month.

BOOK TAG = like normal tag videos but based on books. Answering a series of themed questions and tagging others to do the same. E.g. 'The Taylor Swift Book Tag'.

ARC = advanced reader copy. These are copies of books sent out by publishers for review before the book is released.

DNR/DNF = did not read or did not finish. When someone didn't like a book and so didn't finish it.

TOP 10 BOOKTUBERS

BookTubers are your new BFFs for all things book related. Whether you're looking for a page-turning new novel or all the goss on the latest book-to-film adaptations, this lot are your go-to guides on books of all kinds. No matter what your reading tastes, if you love books just as much as you love YouTube, you're bound to fall in love with at least one of these top channels.

10. JEAN BOOKISHTHOUGHTS

+41K

> > > > > > > > > > > > > > >

NAME: Jean Menzies

ON YOUTUBE SINCE: December 2012

WATCH HER FOR: Interesting vlogs on a variety of books, classical lit and studying.

Jean used to make fashion and beauty videos before discovering the wonderful world of BookTube. Her chatty reviews cover a wide range of books from Greek mythology to graphic novels, fantasy, classical literature and even the brilliant Terry Pratchett and she always inspires her readers to try something new! Jean also uploads some fun non-bookish videos, with monthly faves and vlogs about her uni experience, plus she has an awesome Scottish accent too!

9. BENJAMINOFTOMES

+53K

> > > > > > > > > > > > > >

NAME: Benjamin Alderson

ON YOUTUBE SINCE: September 2011

WATCH HIM FOR: Upbeat YA book chat with lots of recommendations.

British BookTuber Benjamin started his channel in 2012 as a way to share his newfound love of books with the world. His passion for books has grown ever since, along with his steadily rising channel. Ben's love of YA fiction shines through in his ever so energetic book hauls, wrap ups and recommendations. His reviews are guaranteed to put you in a good mood as well as help you find some awesome new books to read. Ben's also recently started his own micropublishing company championing new YA authors, which is pretty darn cool.

Ben is OBSESSED with all things witches and witchcraft.

8. PADFOOTANDPRONGS07

+83K

> > > > > > > > > > > > > >

NAME: Raeleen Lemay

ON YOUTUBE SINCE: October 2011

WATCH HER FOR: Super knowledgeable and honest reviews about books you might not have heard of otherwise.

In case you couldn't tell from her Harry Potter themed channel name, Raeleen is a book fanatic. This Canadian BookTuber keeps viewers entertained with her regular reviews, hauls, reading updates and recommendations, which are funny, insightful and above all, honest. Raeleen is open to reading every genre and is always truthful when it comes to reviewing, whether she loved or loathed them. Her massive book hauls are also likely to introduce you to some lesser-known book gems.

FAVOURITE GENRES:
General fiction, historical, sci-fi, fantasy, dystopian and post-apocalyptic.

"BookTube has changed my life. I've met so many great people and found so many new books."

7. BOOKSANDQUILLS

> > > > > > > > > > > > >

+158K

NAME: Sanne Vliegenthart

ON YOUTUBE SINCE: November 2008

WATCH HER FOR: Short, snappy book reviews and recommendations to expand your reading horizons.

Sanne is a Dutch born, London-based book lover, and something of a celebrity in the BookTube community. Having been in the YouTube game for a while now, every one of her videos is high quality and her books chats always eloquent. She puts her English degree and job in publishing to good use with well thought-out reviews on great books from a variety of genres and interesting insights into the publishing world. As well as YA fiction, she talks about a mix of old and new novels, contemporary, sci-fi, non-fiction and a few classics too. Sanne also stands out for her variety of video content, from collabs with big-time YouTubers to gift guides, London fun and travel diaries.

6. PERUSEPROJECT

> > > > > > > > > > > > >

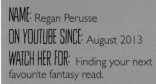

+177K

NAME: Regan Perusse

ON YOUTUBE SINCE: August 2013

WATCH HER FOR: Finding your next favourite fantasy read.

If you love YA and all things fantasy then Regan from PeruseProject is your girl. She reads A LOT, and with both her great taste in books and trusted reviews, you can always count on her to provide some serious book inspo. Her huge book hauls are enough to make any book fan drool, and as you might expect from any good BookTube channel, Regan also has tons of intelligent book chats, fun challenges, bookshelf tours and tags, and she rocks a mean red lip while she's at it.

Regan runs online book club Perustopia with Sasha from ahookutopia! The pair started the club to do read-a-longs with their viewers and chat about their recommended YA 'book of month'.

5. LITTLE BOOK OWL

> > > > > > > > > > > > >

NAME: Catriona Feeney

ON YOUTUBE SINCE: June 2011

WATCH HER FOR: Bubbly book-related content covering all genres, as well as regular readathons.

Probably Australia's most well-known BookTuber, Catriona is loved in the community for her funny, engaging personality and stellar book selection. If anyone was ever guilty of giving us major shelf-envy, it's Catriona. She picks up lots of gorgeous looking books and her book hauls are just beautiful. Her enthusiasm for reading is infectious and she inspires viewers to pick up books they may never have heard of but just have to read. Subscribe to uncover new finds in all kinds of genres, spanning YA, contemporary fiction, sci-fi, manga, graphic novels, fantasy and non-fiction – this girl is certainly sure to spice up your bookshelf.

+164K

When she's not spending all her time reading or creating videos, Cat's busy completing her degree in English.

4. JESSETHEREADER

+185K

>>>>>>>>>>>>>

NAME: Jesse George
ON YOUTUBE SINCE: February 2012
WATCH HIM FOR: Silly, excitable book fun.

It's almost impossible not to love self-proclaimed 'Book Warrior' Jesse. He's not afraid to be weird, and his silly style of filming (including the 'fwoosh' at the beginning of every video) is totally endearing. He is a massive fan of dystopian YA fiction, and doles out eloquent and on-point book reviews as well as a healthy serving of book tags and funny collabs. Jesse is also one-third of the virtual book club called Booksplosion, along with Katytastic and polandbananasBOOKS. The three of them take BookTubing to the next level by hosting monthly readathons and live show discussions and together form the ultimate in #booksquadgoals.

"BookTube has completely changed my life."

BOOKSPLOSION CREW

3. KATYTASTIC

+229K

>>>>>>>>>>>>>

NAME: Kat O'Keeffe
ON YOUTUBE SINCE: February 2009
WATCH HER FOR: Book raves, writing tips and #bookshelfgoals.

When Kat first stumbled upon the BookTube community she instantly knew it was where she belonged, combining two of her all-time favourite things — books and YouTube! Kat's now killing it in the book vlogging world, where she mixes her sarcastic sense of humour with A LOT of fangirling about books, gaining many loyal fans as a result. She talks about all sorts of books, but especially loves YA fantasy, sci-fi, dystopian and some classics too. Kat's insightful wrap ups and reviews will reel you in and provide plenty of book recommendations. Plus, if you're also an aspiring author you should check out her channel for useful writing tips and tricks.

"You don't need fancy equipment, you can get books from the library. The most important factor is a passion for books. If you have that, then you're good to go!"

2. ABOOKUTOPIA

>>>>>>>>>>>>>>>

NAME: Sasha Alsberg
ON YOUTUBE SINCE: February 2013
WATCH HER FOR: Lots of funny and varied content about all things book-related.

Book-o-holic Sasha has quickly become a YouTube sensation with her popular channel, abookutopia. Fittingly enough, Sasha discovered the world of BookTubing after reading a book whose main character was a book blogger! Sasha talks about every aspect of reading on her channel, including book reviews, book-to-film adaptations, trailer reactions, huge hauls, sketches and book events. Her videos are always fun and informative — we especially love her "If you like this then you'll like this" book recommendations and the fact that she gives us #hairgoals with every upload. Sasha reads a lot of YA and fantasy, but you'll also find romances, sci-fi and historical fiction mixed in.

+322K

Sasha now owns close to 1,000 books!

Sasha was an extra in Divergent! You can spot her in the film as an Amity faction member.

>> THE BOOK BOSS

1. POLANDBANANASBOOKS

>>>>>>>>>>>>>>

NAME: Christine Riccio

BORN: 4 August 1992

FIND HER AT: youtube.com/polandbananasBOOKS

ON YOUTUBE SINCE: June 2010

WATCH HER FOR: Hyperactive reviews and relatable book feels with a side of stand-up comedy.

+335K

With over 300,000 subscribers, Christine from polandbananasBOOKS is the biggest BookTuber out there. She's nabbed that title largely thanks to her loud, dynamic personality and sheer enthusiasm for the subject. A true story lover, Christine first turned to BookTube to escape loneliness and to be able to discuss the books she was reading with other people. She now has thousands of fellow book fans as subscribers and has been uploading her hilarious brand of book-related randomness ever since! Her energy and enthusiasm for books and reading is infectious, and she can motivate almost anyone to want to pick up a book. Christine mainly reviews YA literature and fantasy but there is a fair amount of variety on her channel. If she's not interviewing huge authors like Stephanie Meyer, chatting to movie stars or collabing with her BookTuber mates, she's creating crazy comedy sketches and book parodies, fan-girling over Harry Potter and generally making reading fun. So, even if you're not usually a big reader, take a chance and check out Christine's channel – we're betting your TBR pile will soon be sky high.

Christine graduated from Boston University with a degree in Film and Television.

BookTube Tip: "My advice would just be to have fun and be positive… And make sure you're making videos you enjoy about things you're passionate about. If you care about what you're talking about that shines through!"

Christine's writing her own book! She's hinted that's it's going to be a contemporary novel and she's documenting the whole writing process over on her channel!

ONES TO WATCH: The up-and-coming stars to add to your subscription box.

LUCYTHEREADER Teen BookTuber and blogger Lucy loves YA, and we love her! Her high-quality vids are great for monthly recommendations of all the newest titles to hit the shelves.

CHAPTERSTACKSS If you don't really have a type when it comes to books, you'll love Katie for her honest reviews on all kinds of genres. She'll definitely help you decide what to read next.

JELLAFY Jenny has some of the most creative video ideas on BookTube and her editing skills are always on point. We especially love her witty sketches about all the struggles of being a book nerd.

BEAUTY BOOTCAMP

WHAT MAKES A BEAUTY VLOGGER?

When it comes to flawless make-up, hair and nail how-tos, the YouTube beauty gurus are the vloggers to turn to. Whether you're make-up obsessed or a beauty beginner, they're always on hand with step-by-step tutorials and expert advice that's guaranteed to help you feel gorgeous.

30% how-to tutorials

10% hair inspo

100% GORGEOUS

20% hauls & reviews

10% pro tips and techniques

10% celeb looks

10% chatty GRWM

10% make-up faves

THE BEAUTY TUTORIAL

> > > > > > > > > > > >

WHAT IS IT: Make-up tutorials are among the most viewed videos on YouTube. Here, vloggers share their guide on how to achieve all kinds of make-up looks, from celebrity styles and everyday looks to extreme make-up tutorials, where they teach fans how to do awesome effects for fancy dress parties or Halloween.

WATCH IT FOR: A step-by-step tutorial on how to pull off a totally polished look. The beauty gurus show you the products and the tips and tricks you need to recreate the look yourself. Learn how to copy the looks of all your fave celebs, keep up with trends and learn how to use new tools. For whatever look there is to create, you can guarantee you'll find a tutorial for it online.

HOW TO: Tutorial videos usually follow the same format. They show the finished look within the first 10 seconds of the video to get viewers interested. Then, starting from a bare face go through the look step-by-step (usually with a voiceover), explaining the products they're using and how they're applying them; showing viewers how to achieve the end result.

The most viewed make-up tutorial is by transformation queen, dope2111. In it, she shows how to create the looks of Disney Pixar's 'Inside Out' characters, gaining over 130 million views!

TUTORIAL TIPS:

- Try to keep tutorials at around six to eight minutes (or shorter!).
- Be passionate and encouraging. The look should be achievable enough to do at home.
- Use good lighting – whether from a window or studio lighting, these videos need to be well lit in order to fully show off the final results!

- Be creative. Keep on top of the hottest trends and styles and make tutorials on them.
- Some of the most-watched tutorial videos are on a theme, such as Halloween make-up or popular characters and celebrities.
- Engage with your audience – ask what kind of make-up looks they'd like to see next!

DID YOU KNOW? Well-known vloggers are often sent items for free in the hope that they'll give them a glowing review online. In order to keep the trust of their viewers, vloggers should be upfront about which items they've been given. Beauty YouTubers can make a lot of money through paid sponsorships but the very best ones will only talk about items when they genuinely like them – not because they've been paid to.

MONTHLY FAVOURITES

>>>>>>>>>>>

WHAT IS IT: These monthly round-up vids are similar to hauls; except vloggers share the beauty purchases and products they have enjoyed using that month. As well as make-up must-haves, some include other favourite things too, such as homeware, music, fashion and food.

WATCH IT FOR: Recommendations from those in the know. These vids are great for finding out about new things on the beauty scene as well as old favourites, and unlike haul videos, all the items have all been tried and tested. The best beauty vloggers are honest and provide useful advice about products, considering the types of people who would and would not like them.

HOW TO: These videos are great for those just starting out. Line up products within easy reach and talk through them, giving your thoughts about them and the reasons you loved them. Provide links to all the products you show in the description bar. It's also a good idea to wear any make-up products you mention on the day of filming so the viewer can see what they look like on. There are lots of these videos on YT so the trick is to give genuine reviews, include unique things and make your personality stand out from the crowd!

> There are variations of this video where beauty vloggers round up their least favourite items of the month to advise viewers on which products to avoid!

BEAUTY BARGAINS: Our fave beauty gurus use a mix of high-end and drugstore make-up brands to suit every budget, so there's always something for everyone!

GET READY WITH ME OR GRWM

>>>>>>>>>>>>>>>

WHAT IS IT: A GRWM is a combination of a routine video and make-up tutorial. They usually revolve around certain events, like back-to-school, birthdays, nights out or prom, and show the full process of getting ready to go from head to toe, including hair, make-up and the final outfit.

WATCH IT FOR: A behind-the-scenes look at how your fave stars achieve their signature glam looks. You can pick up tips on how to get ready for almost any kind of occasion and since they show the routine step-by-step you can literally follow along at home to create the same look from start to finish. This is a great place to learn how to experiment with new looks and styles and learn beauty secrets from the best.

HOW TO: Most viewers are interested in a vlogger's style and how they achieve it, so film yourself getting ready in real time, showing all the products you use and the rest is up to you! Some GRWM's have a voiceover, some are chatty and some simply have a soundtrack. Most vloggers speed up certain parts of the video (like blending foundation and filling in brows) to keep the video from getting too long.

GET READY WITH YOU

Beauty gurus often prep and plan out their looks prior to filming beauty tutorials. Get creative and use these pages to plan out your own beauty look, planning your colour palette and all the products and tools you'll need to use.

BASE

CHEEKS

BROWS

EYES

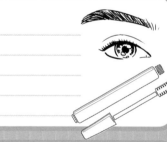

LIPS

TOOLS

Now use colours to
create the finished
make-up look!

TOP 10 BEAUTY GURUS

Thanks to YouTube, there's now a whole host of gurus from around the world ready to help you switch up your look with the flick of a brush. Whether you're looking to learn a new technique, master winged eyeliner or get your brows on fleek, these 10 talented YouTubers will teach you everything you need to know about make-up. Prepare to take your beauty game to the next level!

10. PIXIWOO

\>>>>>>>>>>>>

NAME: Samantha and Nicola Chapman
ON YOUTUBE SINCE: June 2007
WATCH THEM FOR: All the make-up tutorials you could ever want, including an A–Z of celebrity get-the-looks.

Professional make-up artists Sam and Nic were pioneers on the beauty vlogging scene, inspiring many more YouTubers to follow in their footsteps. The sister duo specialise in all things beauty — tutorials, advice, product reviews and a whole lot of celeb inspired looks, including the likes of Gigi Hadid and Adele. From smoky eyes to full brows and make-up mistakes, their 'BASICS' videos are a must-watch for any beauty beginner. The sisters now have a line of best-selling beauty brushes, gaining critical acclaim from vloggers, celebs and make-up artists alike!

+2 MILLION

Kim Kardashian was once a guest on their channel!

9. WAYNE GOSS

+2.7 MILLION

\>>>>>>>>>>>

NAME: Wayne Goss
ON YOUTUBE SINCE: August 2008
WATCH HIM FOR: Top make-up and skincare tips from a pro.

If you're looking to step up your make-up skills, look no further. Self-taught make-up artist Wayne Goss has over 15 years experience in the beauty biz, and now he's here to teach us all the tricks of the trade. Wayne is an expert in breaking down complicated looks into easy-to-manage videos, so his tutorials are excellent even for beginners. From tips on covering spots to teaching how to contour like Kim K, Wayne gets in-depth with techniques so you'll feel like a pro by the time he's finished. He also offers advice on all kinds of skincare issues, from blackheads to under-eye bags. For no nonsense beauty tips and advice you can trust, Goss is the guy to go to.

8. CUTEPOLISH

+2.9 MILLION

\>>>>>>>>>>>

NAME: Sandi Ball
ON YOUTUBE SINCE: February 2010
WATCH HER FOR: Gorge nail art designs you can actually achieve at home.

Bubbly Canadian girl Sandi is super talented at intricate nail art, so it's no surprise she's the #1 nail artist on YouTube! From simple techniques to stunning designs, Sandi can teach anyone how to recreate her cute and easy nail art in just a click of the fingers. Whether you're a total beginner or already a pro, Sandi will have a tutorial to help you nail perfectly painted fingertips every time, using DIY tools and the nail polish you have at home. She uploads new videos every week, with themes ranging from cartoon characters to emojis and current trends, so you'll never be short of some new nail art inspo to impress all your friends.

7. LAUREN CURTIS

>>>>>>>>>>>>>

+3.6 MILLION

NAME: Lauren Curtis

ON YOUTUBE SINCE: August 2011

WATCH HER FOR: All things beauty — from make-up and hair tutorials to product reviews, hauls and how-to advice.

"My approach to beauty is very simple - enhance your features; don't mask them."

Self-taught beauty lover Lauren combined her two favourite hobbies — filming and make-up, to start her own YT channel. Just a few years on, she is now Australia's top beauty vlogger, gaining global recognition thanks to her humble personality and invaluable make-up tips. From bold lips to luscious lashes, Lauren has a make-up tutorial for any occasion, as well as sharing her celeb-inspired looks and honest reviews and advice. As a role model for young girls, Lauren loves to inspire and empower her viewers to be confident in their own skin and to ignore criticism from others. As she says, make-up is all about having fun!

6. TANYA BURR

>>>>>>>>>>>>>

+3.6 MILLION

NAME: Tanya Burr

ON YOUTUBE SINCE: October 2009

WATCH HER FOR: Amazing make-up tips and easy-to-follow tutorials on celeb looks and current trends.

Tanya Burr's channel covers all bases — with celebrity make-up looks, hairstyles, huge beauty hauls, product reviews and all the latest trends. She is a must-follow for anyone looking for some serious style and beauty inspo; she even posts tasty baking tutorials too! We love her easy-to-follow tips, positive attitude and sweet personality, and we're not the only ones — her channel regularly features collabs and cameos from all the popular YT crew. Tanya's online popularity has exploded into the offline world as well, with the launch of her own make-up line, appearances on magazine covers and fashion front rows, awards and two bestselling books.

In 2015 Tanya married long-term love and fellow YouTuber Jim Chapman.

Tanya started vlogging after Jim's make-up artist sisters pixiwoo persuaded her to make her own channel.

5. NIKKIETUTORIALS

>>>>>>>>>>>>>

+5.9 MILLION

NAME: Nikkie De Jager

ON YOUTUBE SINCE: June 2008

WATCH HER FOR: Inspiring make-up challenges and flawless tutorials.

Nikkie is a hair and make-up artist from the Netherlands whose YouTube mission is to share the fun side of make-up and make viewers feel good about themselves in the process. This girl is obsessed with colour, glamour and all things glitter, and she's completely guaranteed to help you up your make-up game. Whether it's how to rock bold colours or wear Snapchat-filter-worthy make-up, Nikkie has lots of tips and tricks up her sleeve that you wouldn't usually dare to try. Her knack for never taking herself too seriously, combined with her incredible make-up skills has gained her millions of fans across the globe. She also sparked an online movement with her viral video, the 'The Power of MAKEUP' — inspiring make-up lovers all over the world to flaunt and embrace their face both with and without make-up.

51

4. KANDEE JOHNSON

+3.8 MILLION

>>>>>>>>>>>>>

NAME: Kandee Johnson
ON YOUTUBE SINCE: January 2009
WATCH HER FOR: Incredible character and celeb transformations.

Make-up queen Kandee Johnson takes celeb-inspired make-up tutorials to a whole other level, actually transforming her face to look like anything and anyone she tries to emulate. From Disney Princesses to Kardashians, YouTubers, cartoons and even Justin Bieber, Kandee's creations are mind-blowing and prove just how much you can do with mad skills and a make-up brush. As well as her transformations and everyday make-up tips, fans love Kandee for her never-ending enthusiasm and positive personality. If you're looking for costume party inspo or Halloween how-tos, Kandee's fun-filled channel will have you covered.

> Kandee used to work as a pro make-up artist for film and TV before making her YT videos.

3. ANDREASCHOICE

+4 MILLION

>>>>>>>>>>>>>

NAME: Andrea Brooks
ON YOUTUBE SINCE: March 2008
WATCH HER FOR: Make-up and beauty tips, life hacks, hair tutorials and easy-to-do DIYs.

American vlogger Andrea Brooks is a pro at giving quick and easy make-up and beauty tips, along with DIYs of all kinds and hair styling hacks. She's basically like the best friend you've always wanted – she'll help you get ready for Halloween parties, teach you how to make DIY hair treatments and she even gives great gift ideas. What's more, Andrea is always relatable and loves to use drugstore make-up products in her tutorials to create a diverse range of looks. With her sassy personality and budget friendly tips, Andrea's channel is not to be missed for anyone wanting to switch up their look for less.

2. CARLI BYBEL

>>>>>>>>>>>>>

NAME: Carli Bybel
ON YOUTUBE SINCE: June 2011
WATCH HER FOR: Friendly hair and beauty tutorials with a touch of Hollywood glamour.

> Carli has her own successful eyelash and make-up range.

+5 MILLION

Carli is one of YouTube's biggest beauty stars and a staple subscription for any make-up fan. Carli's varied channel covers everything from make-up and hair tutorials to product reviews, favourites, fashion, hauls and fitness, so you're bound to find a video for all of your beauty needs. Her glamorous GRWM videos are where she really shines, sharing her on-point contour and highlight techniques and tips on how to accentuate every feature. Carli's even got inner beauty covered too, with inspirational quotes at the beginning of each video to brighten up your day.

>> BEAUTY TRAILBLAZER

1. MICHELLE PHAN

>>>>>>>>>>>>>>>

NAME: Michelle Phan

BORN: 11 April 1987

FIND HER AT: youtube.com/MichellePhan

ON YOUTUBE SINCE: July 2006

WATCH HER FOR: Tips on how to become your own best make-up artist through top tutorials, tips, get-the-looks and more.

Michelle Phan means business when it comes to beauty. As well as being at the top of the YT beauty game with over 8 million subscribers and a billion views, she's now a super successful businesswoman, author and entrepreneur, with her own cosmetics line, a book and enterprises of many kinds – almost too many to mention! Michelle built her empire around posting beauty tutorials, showing her fans how to do everything from DIY facemasks to re-creating celebrity and character make-up, from Lady Gaga to 'Game of Thrones'. Michelle encourages her viewers to experiment with make-up and explore all the different sides of their personalities. With looks ranging from the everyday to the extreme, and with hundreds of videos on her channel, you'll certainly be able to find the look that's right for you. Her signature vids are cool, artsy and expertly edited, featuring her relaxing voice and clear, easy-to-follow instructions. Check out her popular Halloween themed videos for some super spooky beauty tips!

+8.7 MILLION

"I'm passionate about teaching others how to look and feel fabulous in their own skin."

WATCH: 'Skeleton Makeup: Watchers of the Night'

ONES TO WATCH: The up-and-coming stars to add to your subscription box.

KATIE SNOOKS
Beauty blogger turned vlogger, Katie Snooks is sure to be a star. Katie's channel delivers drugstore make-up tutorials, product reviews and ultimate hair envy.

MSROSIEBEA
With a warm personality, wide range of tutorials and gorge ginger locks, Rosie is set to hit the big time. She's recently released her own false nails and lashes line! #want

EMILY CANHAM
When she's not giving us #relationshipgoals with boyf Jake Boys, Emily's busy on her beauty channel providing all the inspo you could ever need!

BEST BEAUTY CHALLENGES

There are lots of fun beauty challenges to watch on YouTube. Some are inspiring, some are helpful and others are just plain hilarious, but all of them have spread across the web. Loads of our fave vloggers have jumped on the beauty bandwagon and tried these ones out – why not try them for yourself?

NO MIRROR MAKE-UP CHALLENGE

>>>>>>>>>>>>>

One of the only times beauty vloggers can get away with rocking a less-than-perfect look is during the 'No Mirror Make-up Challenge'. This challenge sees YouTube stars applying everything from concealer to bronzer, eyeliner and lipstick without the aid of a mirror. The real payoff is when they finally do look in the mirror to see the (sometimes) horrifying results, although most of them manage to do a better job than we do with a mirror. The 'No Mirror Make-up Challenge' has become something of a YouTube fave with many beauty gurus continuing to give it a go and put their skills to the test.

FULL FACE HIGHLIGHTER CHALLENGE

>>>>>>>>>>>>>

Getting in on the current beauty trend for a highlight that's brighter than the sun is the 'Full Face Highlighter Challenge'. 18-year-old beauty vlogger Mariya Lyubashevskaya started the trend when she decided to take the glowy look to the next level by layering and contouring her entire face using ONLY highlighting products! It turned into a challenge once big name beauty gurus, like Jeffreestar and NikkieTutorials tried it out for themselves, each coming up with their own creative yet radiant interpretations. So what are you waiting for? Grab your sunglasses and get your shine on. While your face could end up looking like a glazed glitterball by the end, we kinda love it.

BE A BEAUTY TRENDSETTER AND MAKE UP YOUR OWN CHALLENGE!

THE POWER OF MAKE-UP

>>>>>>>>>>>>>

YouTube beauty guru Nikkie posted this challenge in 2015, and it quickly went viral. She applies make-up to one half of her face and leaves the other totally bare, not only to show what a difference it can make, but also to make a very public stand against all the haters and make-up shamers out there. In the video, Nikkie lets ladies everywhere know it's OK to love doing your make-up; it's a fun and creative way to express yourself! Since then, 'The Power of MAKEUP' has been recreated many times on YouTube and also become an Instagram trend, with people around the world posting videos and pictures and embracing both sides of themselves — made-up and make-up free.

THREE MINUTE MAKE-UP CHALLENGE

>>>>>>>>>>>>

An oldie but always a goody, the aim of this challenge is to complete an entire face of make-up, as well as you can, in three minutes or less. Sounds easy enough, you might think, but it's surprising how quickly three minutes can go. The best thing about this challenge is to see the look of pure panic on the beauty vloggers faces as they realise they're running out of time! Set a timer, grab your brush and try it for yourself!

THE BLINDFOLDED CHALLENGE

>>>>>>>>>>>>

Instead of putting on perfect make-up, here the aim is to turn the tables and have it done as imperfectly as possible. This challenge involves two people, with one attempting to apply make-up to the other while wearing a blindfold. The end results are often messy and always hilarious. Not exclusive to beauty vloggers, many YT personalities have donned a blindfold to complete this challenge, our favourite of which has got to be Dan and Phil's epic attempt, featuring the invention of the beautiful new trend 'ear tinting'. Someone pass the make-up wipes.

WHAT'S COOKIN'?

WHAT MAKES A FOOD VLOGGER?

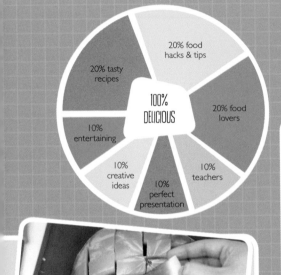

100% DELICIOUS

- 20% food hacks & tips
- 20% tasty recipes
- 20% food lovers
- 10% entertaining
- 10% creative ideas
- 10% perfect presentation
- 10% teachers

It's no big surprise that cooking is one of the fastest growing categories on YouTube — I mean, who doesn't like to drool over delicious-looking food? It's not all recipes, tips and how-to videos either; here you'll find all kinds of food content, from serious cooking tutorials to funny food challenges, entertaining personalities and extreme epic eats. With a food channel to cater to every taste, this is the place to head if you're feeling hungry.

RECIPES & TUTORIALS

>>>>>>>>>>>>>>>>>>>>>

YouTube is now a go-to resource for recipes of every kind. Whether you're cooking for a special occasion or just need some new meal inspiration, whatever you want to make you can pretty much guarantee there'll be a recipe for it. With tutorials guiding viewers through making a dish step-by-step, they are perfect for amateur chefs. Just set your laptop up and start cooking!

TECHNIQUES AND TRICKS

>>>>>>>>>>>>>>>>>>>>>

Food creators can help improve everyone's kitchen abilities, teaching all the skills you need to make delicious dishes at home. There are loads of basic cooking videos for beginners, teaching everything from cooking pasta to poaching an egg. Others show cool kitchen tricks to make cooking easier and more fun, from removing strawberry stalks with a straw to cutting watermelon like a boss.

HOW TO TIPS:

- Successful food creators organise their recipes by meal type, occasion, diet or season to make it easy for viewers to find exactly what they're looking for.
- Titles and thumbnails need to clearly convey what the video is about, since people will be searching for recipe names.
- Make thumbnails deliciously clickable by using close-up pictures of the end result.

WORLD CUISINES

>>>>>>>>>>>>>>

Food channels are also a great way to learn about a new cuisine. They showcase different types of foods and ways of cooking from all around the world.

Cooking with Dog is a Japanese cooking channel hosted by Francis the dog!

EXTREME

>>>>>>>>>

Some cooking channels just go all kinds of crazy in the kitchen, offering something different to traditional cooking shows. From cooking alongside pets to extreme food tutorials and calorific concoctions, these are channels that are fun to watch but you probably wouldn't want to try at home.

BAKING

>>>>>>>>>>>>

Some of the most popular channels are entirely dedicated to making delicious deserts. From cupcakes, cookies, macaroons and cake pops to crazy looking cakes and mind-blowing baked masterpieces, these channels are enough to satisfy anyone with a sweet tooth.

HEALTHY EATING

>>>>>>>>>>>>>

Getting healthy is as easy as watching a video! Many food creators offer lots of quick, nutritious but delicious recipes, and even workout tips and fitness advice too. From healthy vegan recipes to clean eats and gluten-free goodies, there's something to inspire everyone to try to eat healthier.

TIP:

Though there are some professional chefs on YouTube, you really don't need any culinary credentials to start your own food channel – many self-taught chefs are making it big on YouTube. Viewers look for passion, personality, and an interesting twist. Find a niche that plays to your strengths – whether it's mastering a certain cuisine or tapping into a trend.

WHAT I EAT IN A DAY

>>>>>>>>>>>>>>>>>>

As well as cooking tutorials, another popular food-based video is the 'What I Eat in a Day' upload. Vloggers give viewers an insight into their everyday diet with a visual diary of everything they eat and how they prepared it. We love watching these for some much-needed meal inspo!

Use the box below to create your own food diary. Record everything you eat in a day.

BREAKFAST

LUNCH

DINNER

DRINKS

SNACKS

TOP 10 FOOD VLOGGERS

From professionals, to home bakers and food fanatics, YouTube food creators will provide you with cooking advice as well as food inspiration and entertainment. Dedicated to all things delicious, they serve up food, recipes and tasty tutorials on a weekly basis. Check out these 10 channels making a stir on the cooking scene.

10. EMMYMADEINJAPAN

>>>>>>>>>>>>>

NAME: Emmy

ON YOUTUBE SINCE: November 2010

WATCH HER FOR: A food adventure, tasting cuisines and cultures from all across the world.

+811K

On Emmy's unique channel she doesn't just make food – she eats it! Tune in to watch her try food that's been sent to her from fans all over the world. Emmy will literally eat anything, from delicious treats to the outright weird. She's sampled candy from almost every country, space food and even bugs! While her channel is best known as a taste-testing empire, she also includes international recipes and unusual food tutorials in the 'You Made What?!' series. Emmy's videos will not only make you hungry but will encourage you to become a more adventurous eater.

9. KAWAIISWEETWORLD

+886K

>>>>>>>>>>>>>>>>>

NAME: Rachel Fong

ON YOUTUBE SINCE: December 2010

WATCH HER FOR: Pretty sweet treats that are almost too cute to eat (almost!).

Rachel creates the most Instagrammable treats you've ever seen. In case you didn't know, kawaii is the Japanese world for 'cute', and that's really the best way to describe Rachel's channel. After catching the baking bug at a young age, Rachel decided to combine her sweet tooth with her love of all things kawaii, uploading adorable creations weekly. Her channel is choc-full of delectable treats from cat cake pops to rainbow ice cream. What's more, Rachel gives simple step-by-step instructions in her videos, so we can all go completely kawaii!

> As well as baking and maintaining a YouTube channel, Rachel is still at school full-time!

8. POPSUGAR FOOD

+992K

>>>>>>>>>>>>>

NAME: Brandi Milloy

ON YOUTUBE SINCE: February 2010

WATCH HER FOR: Recipes covering all the must-have food crazes.

POPSUGAR Food is the channel to go to for all the latest food trends and crazy edibles. Hosted by the chirpy Brandi Milloy, she shows fans how to recreate food crazes at home and even invents new ones in the 'Eat the Trend' Series. There are all kinds of cool concoctions to make, from giant pizza slices, to cronuts, Nutella burgers and rainbow bagels. There's also a 'Get the Dish' series, sharing easy-to-follow recipes that unlock the secrets behind signature dishes from famous restaurants (McDonalds fries, anyone?). Subscribe for bright and fun videos and recipes that will be sure to impress your friends.

7. SORTEDFOOD

> > > > > > > > > > > > > >

NAME: Ben Ebbrell, Jamie Spafford, Barry Taylor, Mike Huttlestone

ON YOUTUBE SINCE: March 2010

WATCH THEM FOR: Tasty, budget-friendly and easy recipes with a side of banter.

SORTEDfood started as a group of four friends with a love of food, and is now one of the biggest food channels on YouTube. Their millions of viewers play an active role in the channel, since all the recipes are shaped by subscriber suggestions. This makes it a great channel for beginners, as they share a whole load of skills, tips and tricks, as well as hundreds of recipes. In fact, only Ben is a professional chef, so he often guides his mates though the cooking process along with the viewers! With challenges, collabs, and plenty of playful banter, these four will make you laugh. A cooking channel that's both informative and entertaining? Sorted.

+1.7 MILLION

6. NIOMI SMART

> > > > > > > > > > > > > >

NAME: Niomi Smart

ON YOUTUBE SINCE: October 2011

WATCH HER FOR: Healthy eating ideas, recipes and lifestyle inspiration.

+1.6 MILLION

From health and fitness to fashion and homeware, Niomi always gives us #lifestylegoals. While she shares many things on her channel, Niomi's true passion is for healthy living. After overhauling her diet to embrace a plant-based, natural lifestyle, she now shares tips and advice on how to look, live and feel better from the inside out. Whether she's whipping up chia seed smoothies, making sushi or baking healthy banana bread, Niomi will show you how to cook recipes that are healthy and delicious. Her ever-popular 'What I Eat In A Day' series offers healthy food, drink and snack ideas for every mealtime and inspires her fans to eat smarter. If there were ever a YouTuber who could convince us to put down the pizza, it'd be Niomi!

Niomi is co-founder of the health food business, SourcedBox and she even has her own cookbook, titled 'Eat Smart'!

"Creating a meal from scratch using fresh, wholesome ingredients couldn't be more rewarding."

5. JAMIE OLIVER

> > > > > > > >

NAME: Jamie Oliver

ON YOUTUBE SINCE: May 2006

WATCH HIM FOR: Recipes, tutorials, fresh talent, tasty food and funny videos.

+2.7 MILLION

Celeb chef Jamie Oliver has managed to successfully bring his world-famous cooking to his Food Tube channel, presenting lots of his own recipes with all the passion for food and cheeky chappy personality that he's known for. Not only that, he also brings lots of other talented people to light on his channel, promoting some of the site's best cooking creators. There's lots of variety here; each video is fast and fun, showcasing tasty recipes, techniques, expert quick tips and even vlogs giving viewers a glimpse into Jamie's daily life. Plus, Jamie does lots of cooking collabs with all our fave YouTubers too, like Alfie, Jim Chapman and FunForLouis, and even bakes it off with superstars like Taylor Swift!

4. LAURA IN THE KITCHEN

+2.6 MILLION

> > > > > > > > > > > > >

NAME: Laura Vitale
ON YOUTUBE SINCE: January 2010
WATCH HER FOR: Easy-to-follow Italian recipes with a lot of personality.

Laura is a self-trained Italian chef who creates delicious homemade recipes that anyone can prepare. She specialises in making cooking simple, so if you want to master the basics, this is the place to start. With a huge YouTube library of over 1,000 recipes, Laura has every Italian recipe you could ever want to make, from homemade pizza to good old mac 'n' cheese! The big draw of Laura's channel is her friendly personality and informal presenting style. It's this chatty style and superb cooking skills that have turned Laura from a YouTube sensation in to a TV star; with her own cooking show called 'Simply Laura'. She still updates her channel on the regs though, so subscribe for (almost) daily deliciousness.

3. HOW TO COOK THAT

+2.9 MILLION

> > > > > > > > > > > > > >

NAME: Ann Reardon
ON YOUTUBE SINCE: April 2011
WATCH HER FOR: Extremely creative cakes with pop culture themes!

If you love chocolate, desserts and crazy sweet creations, Ann can show you 'How To Cook That'. This Australian baker was a food scientist and dietician before becoming a YouTube star, and her videos really do have the expert edge. She makes seriously impressive sweet dishes, which often don't even look like desserts; with handbags, trainers, iPads and even an entire Minecraft village, made out of cake! We can't get enough of the 'Giant Chocolate Bar' series for tutorials on how to make supersized versions of all your confectionery faves. Though they may look tricky, Ann's desserts are actually very do-able. She provides plenty of easy-to-follow instructions explaining how to make her creations at home. Or, you could just sit back and drool over them like we do.

Ann went viral with her social media themed iPad cake and Instagram dessert.

2. MYCUPCAKEADDICTION

> > > > > > > > > > > > > >

NAME: Elise Strachan
ON YOUTUBE SINCE: September 2011
WATCH HER FOR: Learning how to make perfect bakes like the pros in easy-to-follow steps.

Hugely popular channel, MyCupcakeAddiction, is the world's largest online baking and cake decorating school. It's run by self-confessed 'cake nerd', Elise, who proves that you don't need to be a whiz in the kitchen to make professional-looking cakes. She provides clever tips, affordable recipes and clear step-by-step instructions so that even newbie bakers can create amazing cakes to impress. It's not just cupcakes either; Elise whips up all kinds of confections in her online kitchen. With crazy cakes, desserts, cake pops, milkshakes and character creations, you'll find something special to make for any occasion.

+3 MILLION

WATCH: The 'NO BAKE BAKING' playlist for sweet recipes that don't even require an oven!

>> BAKING IT TO THE TOP!

1. ROSANNA PANSINO

>>>>>>>>>>>>>

+7.4 MILLION

NAME: Rosanna Pansino

BORN: 8 June 1985

FIND HER AT: youtube.com/RosannaPansino

ON YOUTUBE SINCE: April 2010

WATCH HER FOR: Lots of fun and delicious-looking edible deserts based on nerd culture.

When she first joined YouTube, Rosanna Pansino experimented with a whole load of different video ideas before hitting gold with her charming 'NERDY NUMMIES' cooking series. A creative mash-up of nerd culture, baking and Rosanna's adorably dorky personality, Nerdy Nummies soon became a breakout hit and is now the most popular baking show on the Internet. On it, Rosanna whips up all kinds of themed goodies inspired by characters and objects from video games, cartoons, sci-fi, TV shows, books and films. From Super Mario popsicles to Harry Potter milkshakes and Angry Birds cupcakes, there's something to satisfy everyone's sweet-toothed geeky side! Even though Ro's finished creations often look like edible works of art, she's still a self-taught baker at heart, so tries hard to make recipes that all of her viewers can achieve at home. Rosanna also regularly collabs with many big-name YouTubers to compete in crazy food challenges, so it's still a fun channel to check out even if you're not into cooking!

"LET'S GET STARTED!"

Before becoming a YT star, Rosanna's dream was to work in Hollywood. She tried out YouTube simply to get more comfortable in front of the camera and soon enough became an Internet star instead!

Rosanna says she spends 70 hours in the kitchen a week, creating new recipes and testing them out.

MOST WATCHED VIDEO: 'How to MAKE A FROZEN PRINCESS CAKE' - with over 140 million views!

ONES TO WATCH:
The up-and-coming stars to add to your subscription box.

AMBER KELLEY This talented teen is on a mission to make healthy eating cool. Amber shows her thousands of viewers how fun and easy it is to make mouth-watering healthy meals.

LAURA MILLER Laura's entertaining 'Raw. Vegan. Not Gross.' series features veggie-based recipes for people who love to eat. Fans love Laura's quirky sense of humour, slick vids and cooking skills.

DONAL SKEHAN This self-taught cook and TV presenter is quickly on the rise. His channel is filled with great recipes for everyday home cooking, along with plenty of Irish charm and vlogs featuring Max the dog.

BAKE IT YOURSELF!

Below you'll find a simple sugar cookie recipe so you can try your own hand at baking and put your decorating skills to the test. Who knows, maybe you could be YouTube's next top chef.

SIMPLE SUGAR COOKIE RECIPE

INGREDIENTS:
1 cup butter, softened
1½ cups sugar
2 eggs
1 teaspoon vanilla extract
3 cups all-purpose flour
1 teaspoon baking powder
½ teaspoon salt

FOR THE TOPPING:
Coloured royal icing (you can buy this ready-made)

EQUIPMENT:
Cookie cutters

DIRECTIONS:
• In a large bowl, stir together the flour, baking powder and salt.
• In a separate bowl, cream together the butter and sugar until light and fluffy (this will take around five minutes).
• Beat in the eggs one at a time until mixed, and then add in the vanilla. Gradually add in the flour mixture until just blended, scraping down the sides of the bowl as needed.
• Once prepared, divide the dough in half and flatten each piece into a disc. Wrap each disc tightly with cling-film and leave to refrigerate for at least an hour.

• When ready, preheat the oven to 175°C (350°F). Working with one disc at a time, use a rolling pin to roll out the dough on a lightly floured surface, until roughly half a centimeter thick. Use your favourite cookie cutters to cut out shapes, and place the cookies two centimeters apart on two ungreased baking sheets. Re-roll any dough scraps to make more cookies.
• Place the two trays in the oven on the upper and lower racks, and bake for around 12 minutes, until the edges are lightly golden. Rotate the cookie sheets between upper and lower oven racks halfway through. Once done, allow the cookies to cool completely.

NOW FOR THE FUN PART! When the cookies are cool, decorate them any way you like, using coloured royal icing. If you like, you can also add sweets, sprinkles and other edible decorations while the icing is still wet. Set the cookies aside to allow the icing to dry completely: this should take about one hour. Store in an airtight container until ready to serve.

VALENTINES HEART COOKIES

Check out Rosanna's tutorials for some more top decorating tips and inspo or come up with your own creative designs!

Once you've iced the top of the cookie, let that icing set for about 10 minutes before you put another colour on top of it. That way the colours won't bleed into each other.

UNICORN EMOJI COOKIES

Rosanna used unicorn shaped cookie cutters.

If you don't have a piping bag for the icing, you can use a clear food bag and cut a small hole at one end instead.

DIY HOLIDAY TREATS

Rosanna used peanut butter cups to create the hats on these adorable melted snowman cookies.

HOW TO MAKE WARCRAFT COOKIES

NERDY NUMMIES SMART COOKIES

WRECK IT RALPH COOKIES

HOCUS POCUS SPELLBOOK COOKIES

WORLD OF WANDER

WHAT MAKES A TRAVEL VLOGGER?

15% travel tips & guides

10% daily vlogs

10% inspiring

15% culture

100% EXPLORERS

10% travel tales

10% adventures

30% globetrotting

Ever wanted to travel the globe and have amazing adventures in far-flung destinations? Now there's a whole host of travel vloggers who wander the globe for a living and capture it all on camera, making it possible to see the wonders of the world through their eyes. They show us new countries and cultures and best of all, they want to help and inspire their viewers to travel too, sharing their tips and tricks for a life full of adventure.

NOMADIC TRAVEL

> > > > > > > > > > > > > >

Nomads are long-term travellers who are always moving from one place to another. Instead of having one settled place to live, they call the whole world their home! In YouTube terms, the most successful nomads can travel permanently and get paid for it too. Living out of a backpack is definitely not for everyone, but these channels provide us with non-stop adventures, practical knowledge and travel secrets that can only be gained through years of travel.

WATCH: vagabrothers, Kombi Life

GAP YEAR TRAVEL

> > > > > > > > >

Gap years are usually taken either as a break between school and university or between finishing university and starting a career. Whether backpacking, volunteering or working abroad, gap years for many are the perfect time to start a travel vlog. As well as documenting their adventures, these vloggers show how to see the world on a budget and since they are just starting out too, they offer plenty of tips and guides for safe first-time travels, from what to pack to where to go.

WATCH: Hey Nadine, Backpacking Bananas

GET LOST... AND FIND YOURSELF!

DAILY TRAVEL VLOGS

>>>>>>>>>>>>>>>>>>

These travel vloggers capture their daily lives, documenting different places and experiences in a very personal way. Whether they're on the road, looking out at stunning views or just having a laugh with mates, you'll feel like you're on the adventure with them. These vloggers have a strong work ethic and a passion for sharing all that the planet has to offer.

WATCH: Mr Ben Brown, FunForLouis

Successful travel vloggers are able to fund their journeys through sponsors such as hotels, tour companies and tourism boards.

EXTREME TRAVEL

>>>>>>>>>>>>

Full of adrenaline pumping activities, adventure, fun and friends, these travel vloggers go to extreme lengths to showcase the exciting side of every destination they visit. There's no sightseeing or chilling on the beach here — think zip lining, cliff jumping, white water rafting, rock climbing and bungee jumping. These channels make for some super fun vicarious viewing and make us want to get out and live life to max.

WATCH: devinsupertramp, Expert Vagabond

TRAVEL TIPS

Do you dream of travelling the world, making videos and getting paid to do it? Here are some tips on how to set up a successful YouTube travel channel, from the people who do it best.

"You don't have to travel really far to have an amazing experience." – Alex Ayling, vagabrothers

• When you're young, travel can seem daunting but it doesn't have to be. There are plenty of young travel vloggers out there, like Booker from btravelsnetwork, who started off documenting his journeys with family and has been making videos since he was 13 years old.

• If you're not old enough to plan a gap year or save enough money, start by filming your family holidays or day trips with friends. Brush up your filming and editing skills and you'll hit the ground running!

• Here's a fun one – watch as much YouTube as possible! This way you get to know what style of filming you like and what you don't like. There are some really creative travel vloggers out there and watching them will help you learn about editing and you'll soon find your own style.

"Everything I learned about editing and filming is all from watching videos." – RayaWasHere

• Be open to new experiences, whether that's meeting new people or trying new things. Spending time talking to locals and immersing yourself in the local culture of a place will allow you to pick up unique tips and insider knowledge based on their recommendations can make your travel guide stand out from the rest.

• Audio is very important. No matter how good your filming is, if the audio is fuzzy or windy people will stop watching. If you're filming outdoors use wind mufflers and record sound on another device too as a backup.

TOP 10 TRAVEL VLOGGERS

For amazing world eye candy, culture, storytelling, travel tips and an endless supply of info, YouTube travel channels are the first place to visit. Whether it's inspiring you to get off the couch to try something new or going off on your own adventures and looking at the world around you in a whole new way, these ten travel vloggers from around the world are sure to spark your inner wanderlust.

10. BROOKE SAWARD

>>>>>>>>>>>>>>>>

NAME: Brooke Saward
ON YOUTUBE SINCE: May 2007
WATCH HER FOR: Tips, motivation and advice for travelling solo.

Brooke Saward is a happy-go-lucky Australian blogger and vlogger with some very restless feet. On the very same day she graduated from university, Brooke booked a one-way ticket to London and has hardly stopped travelling since! Having been to 50+ countries across six continents all by herself, Brooke's vlogs inspire and motivate other girls to go it alone, showing that travelling solo is not so scary. As well as vlogging her adventures she shares invaluable travel tips and hacks that she's learnt along the way. This girl welcomes every new experience with open arms, and wherever she is the world, you can guarantee she's having a good time.

+34K

"Solo travel is not scary, but like anything it just takes that first leap of faith to get started."

9. KRISTEN SARAH

+95K

>>>>>>>>>>>>>>

NAME: Kristen Sarah
ON YOUTUBE SINCE: August 2010
WATCH HER FOR: Savvy travel tips and adventures off-the-beaten-track.

Kristen is a self-confessed travel junkie who loves to jet around the world and explore new places that are off-the-beaten path – and, thanks to her travel-packed channel we get to go along for the ride! Kristen's vlogs are both energetic and informative and will take you to parts of the world that most tourists never get to see. She provides real-life experiences, interesting how-to advice and expert travel tips, all in her signature comedic style. Kristen's also a talented actress and loves dressing up and acting out her hilarious travel stories based on true events. This is the channel to inspire adventure seekers everywhere.

8. RAYAWASHERE

+128K

>>>>>>>>>>>>>

NAME: Raya Encheva
ON YOUTUBE SINCE: January 2014
WATCH HER FOR: Solid life advice and exploring cultures all over the world.

Bulgarian born Raya is fairly new to the vlogging scene, but she's really hit the ground running, gaining over 100,000 followers in just over a year! Like many people her age, Raya didn't know what to do with her life when she finished university – that is, until she met a cool guy with dreads (hint: he's #2 on this list) who invited her on a road trip across the U.S. and inspired her to start her own channel. Since then, Raya has travelled to some amazing destinations, including New Zealand, South Africa, Singapore, Jamaica, Morocco and Mexico.

7. VAGABROTHERS

>>>>>>>>>>>>>>

NAME: Marko and Alex Ayling
ON YOUTUBE SINCE: October 2013
WATCH THEM FOR: Learning about the world through the people who live in it.

Alex and Marko are two brothers, backpackers and bloggers who are sure to teach you something about the world we live in. Their mission is to explore the globe, from the biggest cities to the most remote villages, seeking out the people who make each place unique and sharing their stories. Their videos are entertaining and educational, full of fun, adventure and useful information, making them a great source of knowledge for any aspiring traveller. These two travellers are always on the go, so subscribe to join the journey.

> Alex and Marko got started after they won 'The Biggest, Baddest, Bucket List' video competition, winning the chance to spend six months travelling across six continents.

6. SONIASTRAVELS

+168K

>>>>>>>>>

NAME: Sonia Gil
ON YOUTUBE SINCE: May 2011
WATCH HER FOR: Smart tips about everything you need to know when travelling.

soniastravels is THE channel to go to for travel trips of all kinds. Sonia shares her adventures, road trips and travels around the world as well as providing expert tips and tricks on how to travel well, in an easy and entertaining way. Sonia will show you how to pack like a pro, how to survive at a hostel, how to budget, sleep on a plane, travel alone, speak to strangers, pick a travel outfit and even how to take the best selfies while you're there. Sonia's is one of the most professional travel shows on the web and her useful knowledge makes it a must-watch for both first time travellers and seasoned pros.

5. HEY NADINE

+288K

>>>>>>>>>>>>>

NAME: Nadine Sykora
ON YOUTUBE SINCE: November 2006
WATCH HER FOR: All the inspiration and knowledge you need to follow your dreams.

Nadine has been in the YouTube game for a while (she started off making comedy skits), but it wasn't until she finished university and saved up enough money to fly to New Zealand that her love for the travelling life was born. Nadine now travels for a living, making videos to show viewers the world as well as sharing tips and advice to show them how they can do the same! With adventures in over 45 countries ticked off her bucket list, it's safe to say this girl knows what she's talking about. Check out her channel for wanderlust travel vlogs, advice and all kinds of hacks, plus videos that'll inspire you and some that'll make you laugh too.

> "Travel has helped me in so many ways… It showed me the world outside of myself, and that's what I hope that it can do for you."

+539K

...ONANDJO

>>>>>>>>

...: Damon Dominique and Joanna
...anco

ON YOUTUBE SINCE: October 2012

WATCH THEM FOR: Major motivation to live the life you've always wanted, stop making excuses and just shut up and go!

Ever wanted to travel but felt like you just didn't know how? If so, this is the channel for you. Damon and Jo are two broke twenty-something best friends who got bored of the same old tired travel shows so took off around the world to create their own, with just a backpack and a few dollars to their name. They've travelled to more than 20 countries, lived in six and have done everything from couchsurfing to staying in hostels and learning from the locals. These two teach how to travel on a shoestring, showing the good and the bad sides of travelling, keeping it real and giving viewers an authentic experience, along with all the motivation you could ever need to get up and go yourself.

> The talented twosome can both speak five languages and upload language lessons so viewers can get the most authentic experience while on the road.

3. MR BEN BROWN

>>>>>>>>>>>>

+645K

NAME: Ben Brown

ON YOUTUBE SINCE: October 2006

WATCH HIM FOR: Destination eye candy, positive vibes and fun times.

Ben Brown is a former professional kayaker-turned-filmmaker who's currently killing it in the travel vlogging game. Whether he's surfing in South Africa, road tripping across California or just hanging out with his mates in a cool coffee shop, Ben's always up to fun things in beautiful locations all around the world. Luckily for us he always has his camera to hand too and shares the adventures daily in awesome vlogs filled with fun, friends and positive vibes. Ben also has some serious cinematography skills – with drone shots, gorgeous scenery and a whole lot of slow mo, it's hard not to get hooked. Watch Ben's 'Visual Vibes' series for stunning shots of some of the prettiest places on the planet.

2. FUNFORLOUIS

>>>>>>>>>>>>

NAME: Louis Cole

ON YOUTUBE SINCE: November 2011

WATCH HIM FOR: Slickly produced videos following the aspirational daily adventures of a travelling nomad.

It's hard not to be jealous of Louis Cole, who has been able to travel the world for a living by turning his thirst for adventure into a huge online following. Creating vlogs from the far-flung corners of the globe, this modern day explorer makes every day an adventure and loves to inspire his followers to get outside, explore and enjoy life. Louis' videos are packed with travel, fun and friends from all around the globe, including many of our YouTube faves. Despite this seemingly chilled lifestyle, Louis is actually one of the most hardworking and committed vloggers out there, filming, editing and uploading a new adventure daily.

+1.8 MILLION

> Louis turned his love of travel into a passion for fashion with his clothing line called 'Find the Nomad'.

> "Peace out. Enjoy life. Live the adventure."

>> NUMBER ONE NOMADS

1. JACKSGAP

>>>>>>>>>>>>>

+4.1 MILLION

NAME: Jackson and Finnegan Harries

BORN: 13 May 1993

FIND THEM AT: youtube.com/JacksGap

ON YOUTUBE SINCE: June 2011

WATCH THEM FOR: A stunningly shot storytelling project inspired by travel.

Jack came up with the idea for his YouTube channel, JacksGap, as a way to document his gap year and share his love of travelling with the world. Jack's vlogs soon turned into a full-time job and began to fund some of his travels. When Jack introduced his identical twin for the first time on camera, his subscriber numbers nearly doubled, and Finn became a co-owner of the channel, adding his design and branding skills to its already top-notch production values. In fact, it's the twins' creative skills and videography talent that sets JacksGap apart from other vlog channels and is one of the reasons so many people tune in to watch. The pair produce some of the most creative and artistic videos on the Internet, sharing documentary style stories about their travels. They've even won awards for their filmmaking and directing skills on 'The Rickshaw Run' mini-series, where they raced across India in a rickshaw to raise money for charity. JacksGap inspire their viewers not only to explore the world, but also, by highlighting the big issues that matter to them, to try to make the world a better place.

"Our aim is to carry on telling stories, exploring new places and capturing the world around us."

Creativity clearly runs in the family – Jack and Finn's father is a TV producer and their mother is a director-turned-scriptwriter.

Finn is currently following his passion to study architecture in New York City.

ONES TO WATCH: The up-and-coming stars to add to your subscription box.

FLYING THE NEST Stephen and Jess are a young Australian couple who started daily vlogging to document their first year of leaving home and travelling the globe.

MOLLIE BYLETT London girl Mollie loves to travel and vlogs about her adventures. She's also a talented singer and often combines her passions in her fun travel footage.

SAM EVANS Aussie dude Sam is a rising star in the travel vlogging world thanks to his crazy cool vids, fun-loving spirit and exposure from the likes of Zalfie. We can't wait to see what he does next.

TRAVEL

WANDER WISH LIST

Feeling inspired to see the world? Use two different coloured pens to mark the countries and cities you've been to and the places you want to visit in the future. Then get planning your crazy adventures!

COLOUR IN KEY:
◻ PLACES I'VE BEEN.
◻ PLACES I WANT TO GO.

"To travel is to live."
– Hans Christian Andersen

DON'T CRY, CRAFT!

WHAT MAKES A DIY VLOGGER?

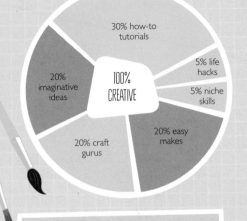

- 30% how-to tutorials
- 5% life hacks
- 5% niche skills
- 100% CREATIVE
- 20% imaginative ideas
- 20% easy makes
- 20% craft gurus

Whether you want a Tumblr-themed dream room, amazing art skills or one-of-a-kind clothes, thanks to the humble how-to video it's never been easier to learn how to do it yourself. From big projects to boredom busters, DIY YouTubers can teach you how to do and create almost anything, using simple steps and budget friendly materials.

ART

>>>>>>>>>>>>

Learn how to draw and paint like a pro with speed art videos, advice and step-by-step drawing tutorials. From watercolour techniques to cool cartoons and realistic portraits, there's something for every art enthusiast.

WATCH: MARKCRILLEY +2.6 MILLION

markcrilley is an American artist, manga creator and children's book illustrator who shares his skills on his awesome art channel. He teaches how-to-draw tutorials on every art subject imaginable!

DID YOU KNOW?

YouTube has over 135 MILLION how-to videos, so you can probably find a DIY for almost anything you want or need!

CRAFTS

>>>>>>>>>>>>

If you're bored and looking for something fun to do, crafty YouTubers will provide you with endless DIY projects to do during the holidays. These channels are sure to inspire your creative side, so get your glue gun out and get crafting.

WATCH: SOCRAFTASTIC +1.7 MILLION

Sarah from SoCraftastic has one of the most creative DIY channels on YouTube. She makes all sorts of DIYs and crafts that you won't see anywhere else, from cute charms to sweet treats, bath goodies, jewellery, duct tape décor and more.

MAKE-UP

>>>>>>>>>>>>>

On YouTube, you don't have to look too far for tips on looking your best. However if you're looking for a tutorial on the more extreme side, you'll find some incredible how-to videos for that too. With all kinds of special effects and downright creepy costume looks, you can learn how to get even more creative with make-up.

WATCH: KLAIREDELYSART +843K

As a trained artist, Klaire de Lys likes to blur the lines between make-up and art in her stand out tutorials. Be warned, these are not your basic beauty looks. With realistic special effects, blood and gore and incredible transformations including real life Disney princesses, creepy characters and each of the Zodiac signs, Klaire's looks are never boring.

NAIL ART

>>>>>>>>>>

Fun and creative nail art has never been easier to achieve outside of the salon. There are YouTube nail art tutorials to cater to all skill levels, from nail novices to nail art masters, so everyone can achieve perfectly polished digits at home.

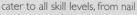

WATCH: SIMPLY NAILOGICAL +3.1 MILLION

With her experimental, one-of-a-kind nail art designs and deep love for holographic glitter, Simply Nailogical is one of the most entertaining nail art channels out there.

Cristine teaches cool DIY nail art hacks and has lots of fun with her inventive designs. She's even down with using school supplies, so get your highlighters ready to create magical rainbow nails.

HAIR

>>>>>>>>>>>>

Hair tutorials come to the rescue when trying to recreate tricky 'dos at home. With tutorials on everything from basic buns to every braid imaginable, there are enough hairdo how-tos to be able to try out a different style every day of the year!

WATCH: CUTE GIRLS HAIRSTYLES +4.9 MILLION

Cute Girls Hairstyles is the #1 go-to channel to learn how to do literally any hairstyle. Mindy has built a huge fan base by showing how to do hundreds of styles, from fishtail braids to buns and updos, including her own creative twists on existing hairstyles too. Plus, the tutorials are all easy-to-follow, with tricky techniques explained clearly, so subscribe for hairstyles you can easily wrap your head around.

DIY

HOME DÉCOR
>>>>>>>>>

Want a Tumblr-inspired room without emptying your pockets? DIY YouTubers have lots of creative decorating ideas to help you get the perfect blogger bedroom, with easy how-to tutorials and hacks to help you get everything you need – from cute fairy lights to candles, stationery, storage ideas and inspiration boards.

WATCH: NASTAZSA +523K

This girl has more DIY Tumblr room videos than you can shake a glue stick at. With fab room makeovers, organisation ideas, simple and affordable interior design tips and on-trend DIY ideas, she can show you how to make the most of any space.

KNITTING
>>>>>>>>>

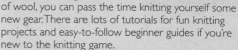

If you'd rather get cosy with a pair of knitting needles and a big ball of wool, you can pass the time knitting yourself some new gear. There are lots of tutorials for fun knitting projects and easy-to-follow beginner guides if you're new to the knitting game.

WATCH: VERYPINK KNITS +199K

Staci from VeryPink Knits is a knitting teacher turned YouTube guru who shows viewers how to crochet and knit anything from blankets and socks to scarves and sweaters. With Staci's super clear instructions, short technique videos and full tutorials showing how to create something from start to finish, you'll pick it up in a stitch.

SEWING
>>>>>>>>>

Fancy being a fashion designer? Sewing specific channels will teach you all the skills you need, taking you right through from threading a needle to constructing all kinds of items, from cushions and quilts to costumes and prom dresses!

WATCH: WITHWENDY +368K

Wendy's channel has all the need-to-know sewing basics as well as cool DIY clothes projects that wouldn't look out of place in your favourite fashion stores. Wendy will teach you how to sew your own clothes from scratch with clear and concise explanations for every project, and you'll find 'How to Make' tutorials for all the latest trends, from bralettes to bomber jackets and off the shoulder tops.

DIY GIFTS
>>>>>>>>>

If you're short on cash or just fancy getting creative this year, why not try out gift-giving YouTube style! There are tons of great DIY tutorials to inspire and teach you how to make original gifts for all kinds of occasions – from Valentine's Day to birthdays, holidays, Christmas, or just for fun!

WATCH: DIYLOVER +791K

Usue's channel is all kinds of awesome. Pretty much any one of her cute and cheap DIY tutorials could be given as gifts, but just to make things easier she has a whole playlist dedicated to cool gift ideas too. From DIY jewellery to panda pillows and colour changing mugs, you're sure to find something to suit any of your loved ones.

PAPER GURU: When you're done making your DIY, check out the Paper Guru channel to learn how to make pretty gift paper and handmade cards, then wrap your present like a pro.

DO IT ALL DIY

>>>>>>>>>>

While some DIY YouTubers have honed and perfected their one particular craft, others like to do it all! These personalities will give you ideas to revamp your room, spice up your wardrobe and even make going back to school exciting with DIYs and hacks for all aspects of life. Get ready for 24/7 creative inspiration.

WATCH: MAYBABY · 5.5 MILLION

Meg DeAngelis, aka MayBaby, is the queen of do-it-all DIYs. Her channel is an array of relatable life hacks and boredom busters as well as all kinds of do-it-yourself projects; from room décor ideas to clothes DIYs and back to school supplies. Meg is always fun, quirky and inventive and never fails to inspire us to get our craft on with her creative ideas. She's even designed her own room décor line, so she must be doing something right.

FASHION

>>>>>>>>>>

DIY fashion YouTubers offer simple guides on how to turn old clothes into showstoppers using only cheap supplies. Learn how to whip up your own slogan tee, tie dye a bikini, turn a pair of tights into a crop top, make customised jean shorts and more. Thanks to their inventive ideas and thrifty ways, fashion DIYs keep us feeling on trend and like we just stepped out of Tumblr — without blowing the budget.

LAURDIY is our fave fashion DIY-er. Turn to the next page for her profile!

IT'S AS EASY AS 1-2-3...

• Do you have creative skills the world needs to see? DIY videos are in high demand so there could be lots of people out there interested to see what you have to teach them! After all, YouTube is the perfect platform to show off your DIY craft projects.

• Since most people are visual learners, it can be hard to follow DIY projects using only written instructions, and this is where YouTube videos can really shine. Make your how-to video stand out from the crowd with clear, well-explained instructions.

• Break the video down into easy-to-follow steps and clearly show what you're doing at every stage, with plenty of close-up shots. Many DIY vloggers use two cameras — one zoomed out to get the whole picture in and one 'hand cam' - a shot that focuses only on what the hands are doing (from above).

MORE GREAT CHANNELS TO CHECK OUT:

• JENerationDIY
• AlishaMarie
• Karina Garcia

>> THE CRAFTIEST CREATOR

LAURDIY

>>>>>>>>>>>>>

NAME: Lauren Rihimaki

ON YOUTUBE SINCE: December 2011

WATCH HER FOR: Quick, simple and affordable DIY fashion fixes to keep your life looking Tumblr-perfect.

Lauren, aka LaurDIY, is a bubbly Toronto-based DIY guru and lifestyle vlogger with a love of ripped jeans, cute sunnies and all things glitter! Her channel is a virtual treasure trove of DIY ideas, from back to school supplies and life hacks to last-minute Halloween costumes, challenges and room décor designs, but our absolute favourite uploads have to be her innovative fashion fixes. If you're after easy tutorials to take your old outfits from boring to brand new, make Lauren your go-to guru. Lauren shows how to look great on a budget with quick and affordable DIY tips to transform any outfit into something completely different. She'll teach you how to turn budget bikinis into high-end dupes, how to make cute new clothes from old t-shirts and how to copy loads of the latest trends for less – basically all the inspo you need to customise your entire wardrobe! Lauren uploads new DIYs every Sunday and with more crafts than you can shake a stick at, her channel has something for everyone. Subscribe and get inspired!

+4.7 MILLION

"I just want to keep making content that people want to see."

"Being unique is better than being perfect."

LaurDIY's millions of fans have a nickname: prettylittlelaurs.

LaurDIY was born out of Lauren's life-long love for crafts and became her passion project and creative outlet while she was at university. She now gets to do what she loves for a living!

WATCH: 'TOP TRENDS YOU CAN DIY'

DIY DÉCOR: INSPIRATION BOARD

Add some YouTuber chic to your bedroom with this easy-to-make inspiration board. Not only will this DIY be totally unique to you and add some wall candy to your room, but it'll help you stay motivated and inspired any time you look at it!

YOU WILL NEED:

- Some old magazines
- Alphabet stickers
- A picture frame (whatever size you like)
- Scissors
- Glue

STEP 1

Go through your old magazines and cut out any pictures, messages and images that inspire you, or print out some pictures from Tumblr. The great thing about this is that you can choose any images to match the colour scheme of the rest of your room.

STEP 2

Once you've done that, arrange the cut outs however you like on a piece of paper (a good trick is to use the paper insert that comes with the frame) until you have a cool collage. Once you're happy with the layout, glue the collage pieces into place.

STEP 3

Now use your letter stickers to spell out any quote or word you like – choose something that is inspiring to you. Stick the letters in place over the centre of your collage.

STEP 4

Pop the picture into the frame and you're ready to hang your inspiration board on the wall!

ADVICE TUBE

WHAT MAKES AN ADVICE VLOGGER?

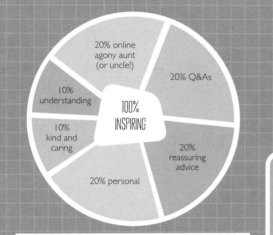

20% online agony aunt (or uncle!)

20% Q&As

10% understanding

100% INSPIRING

10% kind and caring

20% reassuring advice

20% personal

There are lots more useful advice sites on YouTube. The official Childline channel teams up with a different YouTuber every week to discuss big issues, debunk myths and offer help and advice on any problem.

YouTube is often the first place we turn to if we have a question, and it's no different when we have a problem we need help with. YT is a great resource for people struggling with all sorts of issues: you can put on a video and instantly connect with people who have been through the same things you're experiencing and understand exactly how you feel. These vloggers share their own experiences on a range of topics, from serious issues to everyday worries, and offer helpful advice, support and a shoulder to cry on.

DATING

> > > > > > > > > > > > >

The world of dating and relationships can be a tricky one to navigate. Thankfully, our YouTuber pals are on hand to offer some sound advice on boyfriends, girlfriends, kissing, first crushes, heartbreak and all the confusing feels.

WATCH: 'A GUY'S ADVICE FOR GIRLS: DOES HE LIKE YOU?' – Jim Chapman

FRIENDSHIPS

> > > > > > > > > > > > >

They're a massive part of our lives, but friendships can sometimes cause us some stressful situations. From making friends to losing friends, peer pressure and friend drama, YouTubers offer advice that might help you fix your squad probs.

WATCH: 'Dr Meghan: How to Fit In, Find Friends & Peer Pressure' – Meghan Rienks.

CONFIDENCE AND SELF-ESTEEM

>>>>>>>>>>>>>>>

These YouTubers are all about celebrating inner and outer beauty as well as all the little things that make you unique. From dealing with negative thoughts to body insecurities and faking it till you make it, they offer inspiring words and positive messages to help you learn to love yourself from the inside out. They let us know that it's OK not to be perfect – because nobody is!

WATCH: 'How to Feel Confident' – It'sWayPastMyBedTime

BULLYING

>>>>>>>>>

From cyber bullying to school ground taunts, a ton of our fave YouTubers have been bullied at some stage of their lives, as well as frequently having to deal with online hate. They speak out about their personal experiences with bullies and offer their tips on how they dealt with it.

WATCH: 'How To Deal With Bullying' – Marcus Butler

BACK TO SCHOOL

>>>>>>>>>>>>

School can be a bit of a scary time for many people. YouTubers who've been through it all already offer viewers advice on all aspects of school and college, from exam stress to new terms, teachers, revision tips and careers.

WATCH: 'Easy Back To School Tips' – Sprinkleofglitter

MENTAL HEALTH

>>>>>>>>>>>>>>>>

These days YouTube is filled with talk of mental health issues, with everybody from Zoella to Tanya Burr and Grace F Victory opening up and shedding light on some previously little-discussed topics. From depression to self-harm, anxiety and panic attacks, YouTubers are doing an awful lot to help break down taboos surrounding these topics and offer their genuinely helpful advice to young people and teens going through the same thing.

WATCH: 'Dealing with Panic Attacks & Anxiety' – Zoella

While they do make some very helpful advice videos, vloggers are the first to admit that their advice simply stems from their own experiences and they are (mostly) not qualified therapists or doctors. Instead, they offer motivational advice, help viewers realise that they are not alone in feeling a certain way and might even inspire people to seek professional help when needed.

TOP 10 ADVICE VLOGGERS

When we're feeling down, nothing cheers us up more than putting on our YouTube faves. Though most of these channels might not be solely dedicated to dishing out advice, they have a huge positive impact on many people's lives with their inspirational messages, honest chats about their own experiences, and amazing ability to make us laugh.

10. GRACE F VICTORY

> > > > > > > > > > > > >

NAME: Gracie Francesca

ON YOUTUBE SINCE: March 2011

WATCH HER FOR: Truly inspirational vlogs shedding light on the topics that other people don't always talk about.

+211K

Not only does Gracie make videos about fashion, food and beauty, but she's also a total #girlboss, big sister figure, agony aunt and inspiration to thousands of young people. That's because Gracie also talks about serious topics on her channel, such as body image, mental health, bullying, eating disorders and self harm. Grace is honest, warm and above all real, sharing stories about her personal struggles with weight, mental illness and body confidence in order to help other young people. She's like the best friend you go to when you need some straight-up advice — whether that's on what to wear to a party or ways to feel better about yourself.

9. MELANIE MURPHY

+425K

> > > > > > > > > > > > >

NAME: Melanie Murphy

ON YOUTUBE SINCE: May 2013

WATCH HER FOR: Lifestyle videos, vlogs and collabs covering beauty and self-confidence, food, mental health, LGBT issues and body confidence.

Irish YouTuber Melanie Murphy quickly rose to attention after sharing a video about her struggle with severe acne and how she used make-up to boost her self-confidence. She's since continued to talk about more personal topics, making lifestyle videos ranging from mental health to make-up, food to friendship, sharing her musings on life and everything in between. Melanie believes that a healthy mind is just as important as a healthy body and, since talking openly about her anxiety issues, teaches viewers to look after their minds just as much as the skin they're in.

8. ITSWAYPASTMYBEDTIME

+634K

> > > > > > > > > > > > >

NAME: Carrie Hope Fletcher

ON YOUTUBE SINCE: March 2011

WATCH HER FOR: Wise words and heartfelt chats with someone who's already been there and done that.

Carrie Hope Fletcher is one talented lady. As well being a successful YouTuber, she's a singer, songwriter, actress, author and all round lovely person — basically she's like a real life Disney Princess. When Carrie's not busy treading the boards in West End musicals or filming vlogs about her exciting life, she's acting as an 'honorary big sister' to hundreds of thousands of young people who turn to her for her heartfelt advice and friendship. Wise beyond her years, Carrie tackles all sorts of tough topics on her channel such as cyber bullying, body image, insecurities, relationships and growing up. If you're looking for a YouTube role model to follow, it doesn't get much better than Carrie.

7. MEGHAN RIENKS

>>>>>>>>>>>>>

NAME: Meghan Rienks

ON YOUTUBE SINCE: June 2010

WATCH HER FOR: Honest, motivational advice from personal experience – from confidence and dating to fitting in, finding friends and peer pressure.

Meghan created her YouTube channel when she was just 17 years old, filling it with beauty and fashion videos. She has since expanded to include lifestyle, vlogging, and inspirational advice, and is adored for her bubbly personality and positive attitude. However, like anyone, Meghan has been through her fair share of ups and downs and has shared it all on her channel, becoming even more of an inspiration to her millions of fans. So, alongside hilarious Q&As and comedy sketches, Meghan's very open in videos about her battles with depression, bullies and anxiety, hoping to help anyone who might be going through the same things and reassure them they're not alone in their feelings.

+2.3 MILLION

"It's OK not to be OK."

6. JIM CHAPMAN

+2.5 MILLION

>>>>>>>>>>>>

NAME: James Chapman

ON YOUTUBE SINCE: January 2009

WATCH HIM FOR: A very friendly shoulder to lean on in times of trouble.

Ever since finding his YouTube calling in life, Jim Chapman has been uploading chatty vlogs talking to his Internet best friends about absolutely everything and anything, from baking fails to fashion advice. Nowadays, when he's not busy topping 'best dressed' lists, presenting TV shows or sitting front row at Fashion Week, Jim has become known as a lovable big brother figure to his millions of fans, thanks to his #askjim Q&As and 'awful advice' videos where he responds to viewer queries and (contrary to the description) actually dishes out some pretty great advice on all kinds of topics, from dealing with puberty to surviving high school.

Jim studied psychology at university.

You'd never guess it from watching him now, but Jim used to be extremely shy.

5. INGRID NILSEN

+4 MILLION

>>>>>>>>>>

NAME: Ingrid Nilsen

ON YOUTUBE SINCE: October 2009

WATCH HER FOR: Fashion, beauty and DIY videos as well as empowering advice on the big stuff, the little stuff and everything in between.

Ingrid Nilsen first launched her fashion and beauty channel as a means of overcoming her crippling shyness. Now, with multiple YouTube channels and millions of fans, you'd never guess the hurdles she's overcome, but Ingrid gives back what she's gained in the form of honest and open advice on all sorts of important topics. Now totally comfortable in her own skin, Ingrid is your go-to girl for confidence boosting tips and positive lessons in self-expression, as she teaches her viewers how to learn to embrace their true selves too.

"I am giving myself my best chance, and so should you."

4. TYLER OAKLEY

+8 MILLION

>>>>>>>>>>>>>

NAME: Tyler Oakley
ON YOUTUBE SINCE:
September 2007
WATCH HIM FOR: Sassy life
advice and a lot of laughs.

Tyler Oakley is a hero to his millions of
fans for many reasons. Aside from being
a YouTube icon, professional fangirl and
the sassiest vlogger on the Internet,
Tyler is also a total inspiration who puts
his popularity and online influence to
good use by always speaking up on
the big issues he believes in. Tyler is not
only a leading LGBT activist IRL, raising
money for and speaking out on behalf
of gay youth, but he also genuinely cares
about his online viewers and is quite
the life-coach on his channel too. From
serious advice on stuff like cyber bullies
and being yourself, to not so serious pop
culture comedy and hilarious challenges,
Tyler's always a beacon of positivity who
– if nothing else – will probably put a
smile on your face.

"It is crazy what is possible when
you are unafraid to be you."

Tyler has single-handedly raised over
half a million dollars for The Trevor
Project charity. #inspiration

Tyler on cyber bullies: "If it's
happening online, mute it,
block it, don't respond."

3 & 2. DANISNOTONFIRE AND AMAZINGPHIL

+6.2 MILLION & 3.8 MILLION

>>>>>>>>>>>>>>

NAME: Dan Howell and Phil Lester
ON YOUTUBE SINCE: October 2006
and February 2006
WATCH THEM FOR: Funny and absurd advice,
helpful advice and lots of awkwardness.

We simply couldn't separate this dynamic duo –
they're technically always in each other's vids anyway!
People often say that laughter is the best medicine, so if you're in
need of a good laugh to cheer yourself up after a bad day you've
come to the right place. British YouTubing best pals, Dan and Phil,
are known for their quirky sketches, hilarious musings and inventive
challenges, but sometimes they're unintentionally actually helpful
too. While making fun of himself is a key aspect of Dan's channel, he
also touches on a wide range of topics in his Internet rants. With
his 'Internet Support Group' series that "started off as a joke and
gradually got more genuinely helpful" and many tales of awkward
encounters and soul crushing embarrassment, Dan manages to be
both completely hilarious and totally relatable at the same time.
Plus, he also has videos that cover 'how to get out of bed' and 'how
not to survive school', so that's always useful. Phil has built a loyal
fan base for his vlogs and slapstick sketches all about his strange life.
With his sweet and innocent nature and ability to come out with
some cracking quotes, Phil shows viewers who feel like they don't
fit in that it's OK to be weird. The cat whiskers come from within!

Dan and Phil are probably the
two most memed YouTubers
on the planet.

"It's a good thing to be
strange. Normalness leads
to sadness." - Phil

>> THE WISEST ONE

1. SPRINKLEOFGLITTER

>>>>>>>>>>>>>>

NAME: Louise Pentland

BORN: 28 April 1985

FIND HER AT: youtube.com/Sprinkleofglitter

ON YOUTUBE SINCE: January 2010

WATCH HER FOR: Her chatty tone, positive attitude and accessible advice.

+2.5 MILLION

Louise is like the ultimate life problem solver. As well as posting her brilliant beauty and fashion videos on the regs, she's become known as one of YouTube's wisest voices, with fans flocking to her channel to listen to her take on everything from body confidence to boys and being happy. From big issues to small ones, there's no problem Louise can't tackle and she makes sure to keep it upbeat and chatty no matter the topic. Louise's bubbly and confident personality shines in every video and it's not hard to see why she's such an inspiring role model to young women. With her endlessly upbeat attitude towards life, even in the face of difficult times, Louise helps her viewers learn to look at life in a more positive way and feel better about themselves in the process. We dare you to watch one of her videos and not have a smile on your face.

"BEING YOURSELF IS THE PRETTIEST THING YOU CAN BE..."

"Your body is precious and wonderful. Never hide away, never feel less than you are, allow yourself to live joyfully for all of your days."

"ALOHA Sprinklerinos!"

Louise is often joined by her adorable daughter Darcy aka Baby Glitter, and we can't handle the cuteness.

"I feel all the feels that you feel."

Louise started her own Sprinkleofglitter clothing line for plus-size retailer Simply Be and is a big believer in being body confident no matter what shape or size you are.

83

VLOGSPIRATION

"You are beautiful. Don't let anyone tell you differently. Not even yourself."

Although their lives can look seriously perfect sometimes, YouTubers often remind us that everyone has struggles at times. None more so than these absolutely inspirational vlogging stars who have all gone through tough times and come out shining brighter than ever on the other side. Check out their channels and prepare to be seriously inspired.

MY PALE SKIN

>>>>>>>>>>>>>>>>

Em Ford started her YouTube channel, My Pale Skin, back in 2014, sharing her make-up tutorials with the Internet and showing viewers how they too could use make-up to conceal flaws and feel their most confident selves. After receiving so many nasty comments about her make-up free face, Em made an incredibly powerful vlog called 'YOU LOOK DISGUSTING', in which she addresses the issue of Internet hate. The inspiring video resonated with millions of viewers all over the world, and was even noticed by Kylie Jenner, who named Em as one of her favourite body image campaigners.

YESTERDAYSWISHES

>>>>>>>>>>>>>>

Lucy Edwards has a rare eye condition that left her blind in both eyes by the time she was 17, but this inspirational teen didn't let that stop her living her life to the full. Lucy started her channel a year after she lost her sight as a way to keep her passion alive and share her love of make-up with the world. By sharing the make-up tips and tricks that's she's learned since she's gone blind, Lucy goes to show that anyone can do anything if they put their mind to it.

"Every day people say I've helped them and it makes me so happy!"

NIKKI LILLY

>>>>>>>>>>>>

Nikki Lilly is a young beauty vlogger who suffers from a rare and severe facial disfigurement called arteriovenous malformation, or AVM. Nikki has had 20 operations and more than 300 hospital visits for her condition since she was seven, but she hasn't let that hold her back one bit. Realising there were so many things she could do, Nikki decided to embrace her uniqueness and passion for making videos and started her YouTube channel at the age of eight, uploading her beauty and make-up tutorials. She now has over 7.5 million views and 140,000 subscribers on her channel! Nikki's also helped raised thousands of pounds for AVM research and inspires so many people with her positive go-getting outlook on life. What a hero.

One of Sprinkleofglitter's top tips for being happy is to "realise how lucky you are." Take out a pen and jot down a list of the things and people in your life that you're grateful for (not gonna lie, YouTube's at the top of ours). Sometimes it can be easy to let the little things get you down so look back at this page any time you need a little reminder of all the good things in life.

Ten things I'm thankful for:

1

2

3

4

5

6

7

8

9

10

INSPO IDOLS

Cut out and keep these inspirational words to live by – our
YouTube idols can be pretty darn wise at times!

"HANG IN THERE"
– Sprinkleofglitter

"Just say YES!"
– Zoella

"The only thing I'm drinking is body positivi-TEA!"
– Tyler Oakley

"Just know: It will get better."
– Phil Lester

"You are an okay person."
– Sprinkleof glitter

"Keep smiling and stuff."
– Dan Howell

"Be yourself, don't worry about what other people are thinking of you."
– Phil Lester

"Nothing is impossible, even the word spells I'm possible!"
– Alfie Deyes

"Be the BEST version of YOU!" – Zoella

"DON'T give in to peer pressure!"
– Jim Chapman

"In order to get your dreams you need to chase them even if that means leaving your comfort zone."
– Carrie Hope Fletcher

"If you do what you've always done, you'll get where you've always got."
– Sprinkleofglitter

"HATERS, BACK OFF!"
– Miranda Sings

"Stop trying to change yourself just to please other people."
– Carrie Hope Fletcher

"You're all beautiful. And you shouldn't let anyone tell you otherwise."
– Troye Sivan

"Be who you are and say what you feel because those who mind don't matter, and those who matter don't mind."
– Bethany Mota

"Be a WARRIOR, not a worrier." – Tanya Burr

"It's a good thing to be strange. Normalness leads to sadness."
– Phil Lester

"Don't worry about not knowing what you want to do."
– Zoella

"Care less about what other people think."
– Tyler Oakley

BEHIND THE SCENES

There's a lot more to vlogging than just chatting to a camera y'know! Vloggers work hard behind the scenes to make sure everything is perfect; from the camera equipment to the all-important background. A good background setting can make or break a vlog: visually pleasing backgrounds invite viewers in and encourage them to keep watching while bad ones can be an instant click off. Here are some top tips to help you spruce up your background and get ready for action.

ALL WHITE

\>>>>>>>>>>>>

White is the go-to background colour for many vloggers since it looks crisp in videos, brightens up the shot and goes with absolutely anything. Make it look more inviting by adding a pop of colour and some personal touches to your background, such as bright candles, fake flowers, cute mugs and pictures. You don't have to spend lots of money to get the perfect background — there are heaps of easy room décor DIYs to prettify your room on YouTube!

BRIGHT LIGHT

\>>>>>>>>>>>>

Having the right lighting will contribute massively to the quality of your videos. If you can, choose a room or background setting that gets a lot of natural light. Positioning your set-up in front of a big window and filming during daylight hours is ideal — this way you won't need to invest in expensive studio lighting. Just make sure you're not in a position where the sun is shining too harshly on your face, and that it's not brighter on one side of your face than the other, as this can be unflattering. It's all about the angles!

KEEP IT CLEAN

\>>>>>>>>>>>>

Clean and de-clutter your room before filming — even if you just hide it all out of shot! Nobody wants to see your messy room, unmade bed and dirty laundry in the background — not only does it look unprofessional, but it's distracting too and viewers will end up focusing on that when they should be focusing on you!

LIGHTING HACK You can buy a white light bulb to mimic the look of natural daylight. Shine a lamp with a white sheet over it to diffuse the light so it's not too harsh and voila — DIY studio lighting!

PERSONAL TOUCH

>>>>>>>>>>>>>>>

Backgrounds often reflect the theme of the channel. For example, DIY vloggers often have some of the DIY they've made in the background, home décor vloggers will always have their rooms on point, and cooking creators usually shoot in a kitchen setting with the tools of their trade on display. Your surroundings should stay consistent and reflect the tone of your vlog, so add some personal touches to your background that fit your personality, whether it's girly, goofy, crazy or stylish.

Miranda Sings' personalised background full of fan art is instantly recognisable.

FAIRY LIGHTS

>>>>>>>>>>>>>>>

The vlogger staple! Whether they're hung across a bedhead, strung up along the wall or draped along a desk, fairy lights add a warm and inviting glow to any room and will look super cute twinkling away in any background shot.

MyCupcakeAddiction's background is fun and colourful, just like her channel!

Cacti are so cool right now.

KATE LA VIE

MICHELLE PHAN

MICHELLE PHAN

KATE LA VIE

ZOELLA

ZOELLA

#backgroundgoals!

#TEAMINTERNET TIPS

If all this talk of YouTube has got you itching to start your own channel, first check out these top tips and words of advice from the people who do it best!

BE YOURSELF

"I think it's important to just focus on coming across as who you really are because at the end of the day it's personality and the content that's really going to matter. Just get started." – Estée Lalonde

"The best way to stand out and set yourself apart from the others is to not be afraid to be yourself and if that means taking a chance on trying out weird, strange or out-of-the-box ideas, then go for it! Why be like someone else, they're already taken." - Cristine from Simply Nailogical

"Be yourself. Be yourself. Be yourself. I can't stress it enough. You are the only you out there, so embrace it! You're going to be the happiest and the most successful when you're just 'doin' you'! Not only is that authentic for the viewers, but it's going to make you happy. You can't please everyone, that's impossible, so why not just please yourself? " – Meghan Rienks

FILM THE VIDEOS THAT YOU'D ENJOY WATCHING

"Give the world a good reason to watch you... Step back and think 'is the video that I just made something that I would want to watch if someone I'm subscribed to uploaded it?'" – Carrie Hope Fletcher

"This is super important because people get caught up in making content just to get more views. The more fun you have, the more fun people are going to have watching them!" – Alfie Deyes

YOU DON'T NEED EXPENSIVE EQUIPMENT

"Be as good as you can technically… have a decent camera (I say decent, you don't have to spend loads and loads of money on all these things), decent lighting, a good background if you can – I think that really does help." – Samantha Maria

"All you need is some sort of camera, you don't need really expensive lighting and you don't need a DSLR, just sit by a window, make sure it looks kind of half decent and start talking… the quality of the way your videos look is less important than your personality!" – Jim Chapman

DON'T LISTEN TO HATERS

"If you like making YouTube videos and you're being made fun of at school or anything – who cares? Just do it, you like it so don't let them control what makes you happy." – Samantha Maria

"If you desperately want to make videos, and if it's something you think you might enjoy, stuff what anyone else thinks!" – Zoella

ALWAYS BE CONSISTENT

"One of the most crucial parts to building a strong community is being consistent – not just by uploading frequently, but also by responding to comments. It's important to show your audience that you appreciate their support by always interacting with them." – Bethany Mota

"If you create a schedule and people know when your videos are going up, then you can get into a routine and become part of their life!" – Alfie Deyes

HAVE GOOD THUMBNAILS

"Thumbnails are so important. If you don't have good thumbnails nobody will click on your video. It automatically makes your video come off as way more put together and professional." – MyLifeAsEva

COLLABORATE AND MAKE FRIENDS

"The one thing that I've grown fond of on YouTube is making YouTube friends, and this is something that's necessary to do if you want to be successful or just want to have fun on YouTube! Collab videos are a great way to make friendships stronger and work on a project with somebody else and get to know them a little bit better." – MyLifeAsEva

"Tweeting someone with a genuine question is a really good way to get a conversation going… collabs are a great way to get your channel out to another person's audience." – LaurDIY

DON'T BE TOO HARD ON YOURSELF

"You can't expect your videos to be perfect from day one and they won't be… know that it's a learning process and every single video you make will be better than the last one." – RayaWasHere

"As long as you're having fun and trying your best, that's all that matters!" – Sprinkleof glitter

"Do not be afraid to fail… watch early vlogbrothers videos and see that we sucked too!" – Hank Green from vlogbrothers

If you are under 18 make sure you get your parents' permission before making a YouTube account. The Internet can be a dangerous place!

91

THE LOVE LIST

You've seen our top 10 vlogger lists – now we want to see yours! Fill in each section with all the YouTubers you love, to create your ultimate vlogging playlist! This doesn't have to be completed all at once – you can add to the pages as you discover new vloggers you love and keep track of all your faves in one place.

TOP 10 IN FASHION

1
2
3
4
5
6
7
8
9
10

TOP 10 IN LIFESTYLE

1
2
3
4
5
6
7
8
9
10

TOP 10 IN MUSIC

1
2
3
4
5
6
7
8
9
10

TOP 10 IN BOOKS

1
2
3
4
5
6
7
8
9
10

TOP 10 IN BEAUTY ♥♥♥

1 _____
2 _____
3 _____
4 _____
5 _____
6 _____
7 _____
8 _____
9 _____
10 _____

TOP 10 IN FOOD ♥♥♥

1 _____
2 _____
3 _____
4 _____
5 _____
6 _____
7 _____
8 _____
9 _____
10 _____

TOP 10 IN TRAVEL ♥♥♥

1 _____
2 _____
3 _____
4 _____
5 _____
6 _____
7 _____
8 _____
9 _____
10 _____

TOP 10 IN DIY ♥♥♥

1 _____
2 _____
3 _____
4 _____
5 _____
6 _____
7 _____
8 _____
9 _____
10 _____

TOP 10 IN ADVICE ♥♥♥

1 _____
2 _____
3 _____
4 _____

5 _____
6 _____
7 _____
8 _____
9 _____
10 _____

DO YOU KNOW You Tube?

As YouTube has evolved over the years, it's also changed our language and the words we use for things. Whether you're already a fully signed up member of #TeamInternet or new to the YouTube game, you'll never be confused by Internet speak ever again with our glossary guide to what-means-what on the web.

DID YOU KNOW?

The word YouTuber is now in the official Oxford English Dictionary!

AD: Vloggers must be upfront and clear with audiences when they've been paid to produce content promoting a product, service or brand. Using the word 'ad' in the video title and description signals that a video has been sponsored.

AMA: Stands for 'Ask Me Anything'.

CHALLENGE: A popular trend amongst video creators where participants film themselves competing in various uncomfortable or amusing activities.

CHANNEL: A user's own personal page on YouTube, which shows their uploaded videos, playlists, biography, liked videos and recent activity.

COLLAB: Short for collaboration. This means any type of video where YouTubers appear in each other's videos.

COMMENT: A written response to a video.

COMMUNITY: The name used to describe all the members involved in the YouTube world – creators and fans alike.

DAILY VLOGGER: Someone who video logs their daily life.

DESCRIPTION: The box located underneath the video where YouTuber's often leave important links and content relevant to the video.

FANDOMS: The collective name for a group of fans. There are many different fandoms in the YouTube world, each with their own name e.g. Sugglets, Mirfandas, etc.

FAVOURITES: A monthly video breakdown of a YouTuber's favourite items or products.

FEATURED VIDEO: A video that has been selected to automatically play when you click onto a YouTuber's channel page. Often this will be a trailer showcasing what the channel is all about.

GRWM: Stands for Get Ready With Me.

HAUL: A popular video where creators show viewers the items they've recently purchased.

LET'S PLAY: A very popular style of gaming video where viewers watch a YouTuber playing a video game, usually with voice-over commentary.

MEME: An image, activity, video or catchphrase that is copied and spread rapidly from person to person via the Internet, often with slight variations.

OOTD: Stands for Outfit Of The Day.

OTP: Stands for One True Pairing. Used to describe two people who you think would make the perfect couple.

PLAYLIST: A collection of videos that can be created using any videos on YouTube. It's a good way of organising content and can also be easily shared with others.

PHANDOM: The fandom name for fans of popular YouTubers Dan and Phil. You are likely to encounter the Phandom if you spend any time at all in the YouTube comments sections.

Q&A: A simple sit-down question and answer video format used by many YouTubers.

RL: stands for Real Life. The place that you occasionally have to return to after binge watching YouTube videos for hours.

SHIP: Short for relationship, to 'ship' is to support or endorse a romantic relationship between two people.

SUBSCRIBER: A YouTube user who is subscribed to another user. Subscribers get automatic updates whenever a new video is posted and will also see that channel's activity in their homepage feed.

TAG: A video in which someone completes a themed challenge or set of questions and then 'tags' other people to do them too.

TROLL: A person who deliberately causes controversy in an online setting, and who is best off ignored and reported.

TUTORIAL: A step-by-step guide showing viewers how to do or make something.

THUMBNAILS: A small picture that represents each video on YouTube

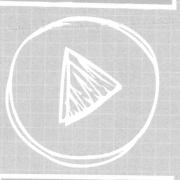

UNBOXING: A hugely popular Internet trend where people film themselves opening or unpacking a new product for the first time.

VINE: A social media app where users post short six-second video clips. In October 2016 Vine announced it would be closing. Viners won't be able to post new content, but luckily the website will remain active so we can still enjoy all the hilarious Vines.

VINERS: Someone who uses and uploads to the Vine app. There is some crossover between Viners and YouTubers, as more and more Viners begin to use YouTube too.

VIRAL: A piece of content (YouTube video, Vine, blog article, photo, etc.) that has rapidly become very popular. This often occurs thanks to word of mouth and the frequent sharing of one particular piece of content all over the Internet.

VLOG: Video blog. A conversational video format featuring a person talking directly to camera.

VLOGGER: Any individual who documents their life, thoughts, opinions and interests in video form on YouTube.

VLOGMAS: The time of year where YouTubers take on the challenge of vlogging and uploading festive footage every day in the run-up to Christmas Day.

YOUTUBE: The most popular video-sharing site on the web.

YOUTUBER: A frequent user of the YouTube website, particularly someone who produces and appears in videos for the purpose of entertaining or informing others. YouTubers can span from comedians to gamers, musicians to vloggers and much more!